GHOST SHIPS

GHOST
SHIPS

TALES OF
ABANDONED,
DOOMED AND
HAUNTED
VESSELS

GREENWICH
EDITIONS

Angus Konstam

This edition published in 2005 by
Greenwich Editions
The Chrysalis Building
Bramley Road, London W10 6SP

An imprint of **Chrysalis** Books Group plc

Produced by
PRC Publishing
The Chrysalis Building
Bramley Road, London W10 6SP

An imprint of **Chrysalis** Books Group plc

ISBN 0 86288 738 0

Printed and bound in China

Picture Acknowledgements

T=Top B= Bottom C= Centre R=Right L=Left.

© Alamy Images: © Popperfoto/Alamy(A4E179): p119,
©Geogphotos/Alamy (AA9287): p121.
© Australian War Memorial [304068]: p71.
© Chrysalis Image Library: p21, p22, p23T, p24, p33, p36, p37, p39,
p49, p60, p63, p79, p87, p97, p109, p118, p123, p140.
© CORBIS: p17, p55. / © Richard Cummins/CORBIS p11. ©
Bettmann/CORBIS p13, © Hulton-Deutsch Collection/CORBIS
p46, © Bettmann/CORBIS p88, p93.
© Digital Vision p8, p74.
Courtesy Emlyn Brown: p101, p103, p106.
© Erik Jensen collection, www.skoleskibet-koebenhavn.dk: p69, p70.
© Fortean Picture Library: p62, p85.
Library of Congress, Prints & Photographs Division: [LC-DIG-
ggbain-04906] p7T, [LC-USZ62-69274] p7B, [LC-USZC4-8768]
p10, [LC-USZ62-65466] p12, [LC-USZ62-105526] p16, [LC-
USZ62-64957] p18,[LC-USZ62-76929] p19T, [LC-DIGggbain-
00081] p20, [LC-USZ62-118048] p25T, [LC-USZ62-24662] p25B,
[LC-USZC4-1752] p26, [LC-DIG-cwpb-01513] p27, [LC-DIG-
ggbain-09667] p28, [LC-USZ62-26149] p29, Detroit Publishing
Company Collection [LC-D4-20520] p31, [LC-USZ62-92666] p32,
[LC-USZ62-52104] p45, [LC-USZC2-3556] p48, [LC-USZ62-
71035] p53, [LC-USZ62-71036] p54, [LC-USZ62-50670] p77,
[HABS, FLA,44-KEY,17-1] 94, [LC-GIG-ggbain-09976] p95, [LC-
DIG-ggbain-09708] p138.
© Mary Evans Picture Library: p83.
Courtesy of National Museums Liverpool (Merseyside Maritime
Museum): p42, p61T, p61B.
© Stratford Archive: p15, p23B, p34, p35, p40, p44, p47, p51, p56,
p58, p59, p64, p65, p66, p68, p81, p92, p99, p105, p107, p110, p111,
p113, p115, p117, p125, p127, p128, p131.
© Topfoto: p82, p91. / ©Topfoto/Fotomas p6. / © 2004
Fortean/TopFoto p137.
© US Navy Photo p41, p73, p74.

Chrysalis Books Group Plc is committed to respecting the intellectual
property rights of others. We have therefore taken all reasonable
efforts to ensure that the reproduction of all content on these pages is
done with the full consent of copyright owners. If you are aware of
any unintentional omissions please contact the company directly so
that any necessary corrections may be made for future editions.

CONTENTS

INTRODUCTION

From Wagner to Wordsworth, Homer to Hollywood, the notion of the ghost ship has long caught the imagination of the public, and provided art and literature with a suitably mysterious theme. One of the most recent examples is the film *Ghost Ship* (2002), directed by Steve Beck, where a salvage crew discover a passenger ship which supposedly went missing in 1962 still afloat in the remote Bering Sea. As they try to tow her back to port, the malevolent spirits which roam the ship try their best to prevent the salvage team from reaching the safety of the shore. This theme—first used by Homer in *The Odyssey*—has been a popular literary device ever since. This popularity reflects our abiding interest in two linked phenomenon; mysteries of the sea and inexplicable, apparently supernatural events.

Mankind has long had a morbid fascination with the mysteries of the sea. Stories of phantom ships, mysteriously abandoned vessels, and tales of unexplained disappearances on the high seas have circulated for as long as man has sailed the oceans. Probably the most famous phantom ship story is that of the Flying Dutchman. According to legend, a 17th-century Dutch sea captain was caught in a terrifying storm off the Cape of Good Hope. As a punishment for blaspheming and tempting fate, he was condemned to relive his ordeal through all eternity. Reputedly, any mariner who encountered the Flying Dutchman and his phantom ship was also destined to meet a grim fate. The legend served as the theme for a Wagner opera, and has been retold in various ways ever since.

Phantoms, and even phantom ships, can often be explained as being the result of optical illusions. Mariners who encounter ghost ships may be simply witnessing a mirage caused by the refraction of light rays, and the old tales are resurrected as a means of

Right: The notion of ghost ships combines our fascination with the power of the sea, shipwrecks, and maritime superstition to produce an image which is powerful enough to seem real to generations of mariners. Even hardened U-boat commanders and naval officers have claimed to have encountered the Flying Dutchman. Did these men invent such tales, or is there more to the legend than can be rationally explained?

explaining what they saw. However, a string of eminently reputable witnesses claimed to have seen the Flying Dutchman, including the future King George V. Other less famous phantoms and ghosts have been reported by hard-bitten mariners and sea captains whose reputation makes them impeccable witnesses; these men would have recognized a mirage when they saw one. While many appearances of maritime ghosts and ghost ships have rational explanations, others do not, and so remain perplexing and disturbing mysteries.

Since the *Mary Celeste* was found drifting and abandoned in 1877, the public imagination has been gripped by tales of ships being inexplicably abandoned. Apart from the tangible evidence of the abandoned vessel itself, there was often very little evidence left behind which could explain what happened. In other cases the clues were confusing or contradictory. In a few examples, this evidence may have explained part of the story, but left important questions unanswered. Such is the abiding fascination of sea mysteries that there is never any shortage of theories to help explain what might have happened, ranging from the highly probable to the downright incredible.

The aim of this book is not to provide a catalogue of every unsubstantiated ghost story associated with the sea, or a list of every ship which disappeared under seemingly mysterious circumstances. Rather it is to gather together some of the most enduring stories of ghost ships, nautical mysteries or inexplicable events, and to present the evidence as impartially as possible. I freely admit that I am highly skeptical of any

Above: While a young midshipman serving on HMS *Bacchante* in 1884, the future George V recorded that the Officer of the Watch and the lookouts had all seen the Flying Dutchman.
Below: The persistence of tales of ghost ships among mariners suggests a strongly-held superstitious belief, but the occasional sighting by onlookers on land is harder to rationalize.

Ye Ghoſt Ship

suggestion of supernatural forces at work. Therefore I have attempted to dismiss the more outlandish claims and unsubstantiated sightings of ghosts or ghost ships. The same sifting process had been applied to nautical mysteries or accounts of doomed ships and other cases where there is some doubt as to the cause of a maritime disaster. This means that several well-known ghost stories or accounts of vessels which sank under mysterious circumstances have been left out of this book. By stripping away those cases where an accident is readily explicable, or an account of a ghostly sighting lacks corroborative evidence, then the reader is left with a series of accounts which are even more fascinating. After uncovering all the evidence he can, even the highly-skeptical author has been forced to admit that some of these events simply defy logic. Please join me on my investigative journey into some of the most abiding and perplexing mysteries of the sea.

Right: To non-mariners the sea may seem a mysterious place, and venturing beyond the safe confines of land could be seen as tempting fate.

SUPERSTITION
AND THE SEA

SAILORS' SUPERSTITIONS
AND THE POWER OF THE SEA

By tradition sailors are seen as notoriously superstitious. While this is less true today in the age of radar, satellite navigation, and accurate weather tracking, many of the old superstitions still manage to persist. These include not whistling while at sea, as this could incite a storm, or the old argument that changing the name of a ship can only bring bad luck. In Robert Louis Stevenson's *Treasure Island*, cabin boy Jim Hawkins is informed about the fate of a pirate acquaintance of Long John Silver, a former shipmate of the notorious pirate Bartholomew Roberts: "He was hanged like a dog, and sun-dried like the rest, at Corso Castle. That was Roberts' men, that was, and comed of changing names to their ships—*Royal Fortune*, and so on. Now what a ship was christened, so let her stay, I say."

Above: According to sailors' superstition during the age of sail, it was tempting fate to whistle on board ship as the act might "whistle up a storm."

Many of the old superstitions were designed to protect mariners from unexpected dangers at sea during the age of sail, so it is a tribute to the nature of sailors that such superstitions still linger on today. Friday is still held as a bad day for a ship to begin a voyage, a bottle is still broken across the bow of a ship when it is launched, and flowers carried on board are still seen by some to be unlucky, as they could be destined to form part of a wreath for a future death on board. Priests are regarded as unlucky on board ship, while women are seen as unlucky unless they are naked to the elements—a sight which is meant to help calm the storm and explains why so many figureheads from the days of sail featured the image of a bare-breasted woman.

Some older superstitions are more sinister. It was once held that, in order to bless a ship, blood had to be spilt on her keel during her launch. Legend has it that the ancient Phoenicians tied slaves to their slipways, so they would be crushed when a galley was launched, thereby bestowing upon it a blessing of good luck. Similar examples of sacrifice can be found in the literature of the Norsemen. Many of these older superstitions may have had a root in ancient mythology, where certain actions were designed to appease the gods, while others could incite their wrath. The Greek god Poseidon (known as Neptune by the Romans), son of Cronos and Rhea, lord and ruler of the sea, was supposed to live in a palace at the bottom of the Aegean

Above: Figureheads reflected the superstition of mariners as they were totems of good luck. Depictions of bare-breasted women were seen as being particularly lucky.

Sea, off Euboea. The god of the sea was attributed the power to gather storms and create tidal waves but, if he was appeased, he could also pacify the waves, and even grant a safe passage to mariners who paid homage to him. This ability to be both a protector and a deadly threat to ancient mariners may well account for the positive and negative aspects of many sailor's superstitions which still exist today. For example, while whistling is generally seen as unlucky as it could "whistle up" a storm, whistling during a dead calm is seen as beneficial, as it could lead to a good sailing wind. Once the ship is no longer becalmed, it becomes unlucky again.

Given the natural elements the mariner has to deal with, it is little wonder that he is superstitious. The oceans of the world (Pacific, Atlantic, Indian, Arctic, and Southern) and the numerous seas (including the Caribbean, Mediterranean, and South China Seas) account for 70 percent of the surface area of the planet. The Atlantic Ocean alone consists of over 64 million square miles (166 million sq. km) of sea. More is known now of the nature and effect of winds, ocean currents, and tides, but we are far from being fully knowledgeable of the way different natural factors react with the ocean. Even in the age of weather satellites and storm tracking, we cannot predict the course of a tropical storm, a hurricane or a typhoon with flawless accuracy. How much harder was it to predict these storms during the age of the sailing ship, or even before the launch of the first satellite? The seas remain an unpredictable and potentially hostile environment, regardless of the large number of ships which safely traverse them. The powers of this environment should never be underestimated; even in the modern age, with the latest technology at our disposal, slight changes in wind and sea state can be the prelude to the onslaught of an unexpected storm of terrifying ferocity. For many the sea remains a place of mystery, of foreboding: we are still unsure of what natural calamities can befall us on the oceans, or even of what creatures lurk beneath its surface. Many of the mysteries of the sea, the legends of ghost ships, and the tales of vanishing ships are made all the more fascinating because they are set against an environment which we will never fully understand.

SEA MONSTERS

By the 21st century mankind had traversed virtually every part of the world's oceans. However, much of what lies beneath remains something of a mystery. While oceanographers have mapped the salient features of the world's seabeds, only a tiny fragment of this large expanse has been explored. It may be difficult to believe that living creatures could survive in the coldest, darkest parts of the world's major oceans, but recent research has shown that these regions are brimming with numerous forms of life. New species of marine life are being discovered every year. It seems little wonder that we remain uncertain exactly what creatures we might find in the sea. For centuries, sailors have reported seeing strange sea creatures, and even wilder tales circulated of ships being pulled under by them, or being devoured. While many of these accounts may be bogus, we now know that some of the sea creatures witnessed by mariners of old might well have been real. Over the past few decades a number of deep-sea creatures have been discovered that were long thought to be extinct, or whose existence was never suspected. Strangely, several of these are similar to the creatures used to illustrate ancient maps and charts. What was long thought to be mythical embellishment might well have a basis in fact. For example, in 1976 the US Navy managed to accidentally snare a hitherto unknown species of shark in the Pacific Ocean. The creature weighed just over a ton, and had such an unusual array of teeth it was dubbed "megamouth." Another similar shark was caught off the Philippines in 1998. If new species of sharks are out there, what else could be lurking beneath the water?

Right: The description given to sea monsters may have varied on occasion, but many fell into two main categories; the sea serpent (depicted here) and the giant octopus. This sea serpent was sighted by the crew of the warship HMS *Daedalus* as it sailed off the African coast in 1848. According to witnesses it measured over 60 feet long, and moved close past the ship at a speed of around 15 knots.

THE SEA-SERPENT WHEN FIRST SEEN FROM H.M.S. "DÆDALUS."

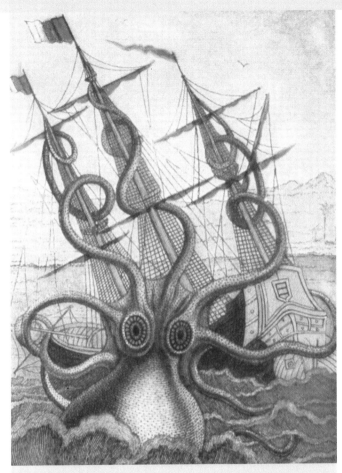

Above: The great octopus and great squid may have existed, but no real creature was as large as the tentacled sea creature portrayed in this 17th-century engraving.

Many old tales of sea creatures refer to giant tentacled creatures resembling squid or octopus. In 1997, marine scientists found the remains of a giant squid in the Caribbean which appeared identical to those illustrated in old sea charts. The Bahamians have long spoken of a sea creature they call the "lusca," a form of giant octopus. Its description closely matches the "kraken," another semi-legendary creature which appears in numerous tales about monsters of the deep. According to legend its tentacles could stretch as high as the masthead of a sailing ship, and if the ship were attacked the kraken would wrap its tentacles around the vessel and pull it under or cause it to capsize. Norse sagas dating from the 12th century mention a kraken "the size of an island," while later accounts might have reduced the size of the monster, but made it no less deadly. Similar creatures have been recorded in the waters of the Mediterranean and the Indian Ocean by 16th-century mariners.

In 1896 the upper body of a giant octopus-like creature washed ashore on the beach of St. Augustine, Florida. A local naturalist recorded what he saw. The section of unidentified sea creature was over 21 feet (6.4 m) long and six feet (1.8 m) in diameter, had a thick skin, and weighed over six tons. Samples were sent to the Smithsonian Institution in Washington D.C., but at first they refused to consider the possibility that it was anything other than a decomposed whale. It wasn't until the 1970s that the samples were re-examined using modern scientific techniques: it was discovered that the cells of the creature were completely unlike those of a whale, and more closely resembled the octopus. More surprisingly, it suggested that the original octopus would have been over 150 feet (46 m) long, including tentacles.

The lusca is a creature that the people of the Bahamas have seen for years. It matches the description of a giant octopus but is it possible that such a creature could exist? Are the remains mentioned above really from a unknown species of giant octopus? We know that giant squids *do* exist, but it has never been confirmed that giant octopuses do. According to some marine scientists, the octopus would be more likely to attack ships and sailors than a squid would, so if there is a giant variety of the species, this could add credibility to stories of giant squid or octopuses attacking ships. The kraken, as seen by thousands of sailors, was a sea serpent but its description matches that of the giant squid. How many "kraken" attacks were the work of a giant octopus? The corpses of "luscas" have been recovered in the Bahamas, and resemble smaller versions of this giant octopus. Does this mean the kraken really exists somewhere in the deeper recesses of the oceans?

In 1997 marine biologists found the body of a giant squid, a creature that was often thought to be the stuff of myth. While they had been seen before, few believed they actually existed. A well-documented sighting took place in 1861, when the French steamer *Alecton* encountered just such a creature off the Canary Islands. Harpoons were fired at the creature, and attempts to harness it failed, although part of its tail or tentacle was recovered and sent to the Academy of Sciences in Paris. The scientists declared it a hoax, as such a creature did not exist: clearly they were wrong. Other sightings followed, and eventually scientists accepted the existence of the giant squid (genus *Architeuthis*). They are carnivorous mollusks, with beak-like mouths, long, torpedo-shaped bodies, and five pairs of tentacles, one pair smaller than the rest. Even today little is known about these creatures, but we do know they can be ferocious. One account, recorded in 1966 by two South African lighthouse keepers, described how they watched a giant squid attack a baby whale, and after a struggle the squid managed to pull it beneath the waves. Could a larger version of one of these creatures be capable of threatening a ship? Are these giant squids and giant octopus-like creatures the kraken of legend?

After all, scientists believed the prehistoric fish they call a coelacanth had been extinct for 400 million years before one was recovered from the Indian Ocean in 1938. This fish which pre-dated the dinosaurs was still thriving deep in the waters off the African coast. Maritime history is littered with accounts of the sightings of strange undersea creatures, from the account of St. Columba who claimed he saw a monster in Loch Ness, Scotland, in AD 565, to the recent sightings of a creature in Chesapeake Bay (nicknamed "Chessie" by the press) as recently as 2002. A seemingly identical creature to both "Chessie" and "Nessie" is the "sea monster" reportedly sighted at intervals off the coast of Oregon known as "Claude." Are these just examples of wishful thinking, or do hitherto-unrecorded sea creatures exist? Apart from the "megamouth" shark discovered in 1976, other new species of marine creatures discovered over the past 50 years include the cochoto porpoise (1958), the Japanese beaked whale (1958), and the Prudes Bay killer whale (1983). It is entirely possible that other mysterious sea creatures are lurking out there, just waiting to be identified.

Above: Mythical sea monsters depicted attacking passing ships in the North Atlantic waters between Iceland and the Faroes. This artwork reflected the fears of everyday mariners in the age of discovery and exploration. Detail from the mid-16th century Carta Olaus Magnus (Tankerness House Museum, Kirkwall, Orkney).

DOOMED VESSELS

UNLUCKY SHIPS

The notion that some ships are unlucky, or are fated to sink is not new, but an idea which has existed for centuries. A long-held superstition of mariners is that ships can develop personalities, and that vessels and their crews can be dogged by associated bad luck, or worse. It is connected to the notion that re-naming a ship is unlucky. According to superstition, the name of every vessel is recorded in Poseidon's (or Neptune's) "Ledger of the Deep." In the same register are listed the names of ships which have offended the God of the Sea, and it records that he has placed a curse on the ship.

Some of the ships mentioned in this book developed a reputation for being unlucky: the RMS *Oceanic* and the SS *Great Eastern* being just two examples. The German battleship *Tirpitz* was regarded as being unlucky, while the battle cruiser *Scharnhorst* was considered lucky. Clearly this is subjective, as both ships were sunk with large loss of life. Certain types of vessels such as submarines are more prone to the vagaries of chance than others, as they are more likely to suffer from serious accidents while diving than a surface warship would.

Then there is the notion that some vessels are not just unlucky, but are actually doomed. A perfect example of this was the World War I German submarine UB-65, which was plagued by such a string of accidents and fatalities that her crew considered their ship to be haunted. The following examples are intended to demonstrate that ships may be unfortunate, or they might be lost in tragic circumstances, but in most cases there is some logical explanation for it. It will also show that, in a small number of cases, there seems to be no logical explanation for the accident or tragedy. Possibly sailors might have a point: can certain vessels be unlucky, or ships be regarded as doomed vessels?

Right: The "calamitous titan" the SS *Great Eastern* was a marvel of engineering but when first launched in 1857, the winch controlling the launch slipped and spun free, killing one man and injuring several others. For the rest of her career, the largest ship of her age was plagued by a series of accidents and shadowed by tales of supernatural encounters.

Below: An image of the German battlecruiser, the *Scharnhorst*, taken in 1939. Nautical superstition surrounded this vessel and although she was eventually sunk, she was considered to be a lucky ship.

LADIES OF THE OCEAN:
DOOMED LINERS

Probably the most impressive vessels ever to take to the sea, the great stately liners of the first decades of the 20th century were the ultimate in maritime luxury. They also seemed to be accident prone, or as one writer put it, "touched by the hand of fate."

During the last years of the 19th century the most prestigious transatlantic liner was the Royal Mail Ship (RMS) *Oceanic*, launched in Belfast in January 1899. Her construction had been part-subsidized by the British Admiralty so that in time of war she could be quickly and easily converted into a high-speed auxiliary warship. Though far from ideal, the doctrine of the time was that, in extremis, ships of this kind could protect the seas from commerce raiders, or even hunt down submarines. The 17,200-ton liner was owned by the White Star Line, and her opulence earned her the nickname the "White Star's Millionaires' Yacht." At 704 feet (216 m) long she was also the first ship in the world to exceed the length of Isambard Kingdom Brunel's SS *Great Eastern*, built a half century before. Her maiden voyage took place in September 1899; although not the fastest liner, she was the most luxurious—and she was also unlucky. In September 1901 she rammed and sank the British coaster S.S. *Kincora* in heavy fog. A mutiny by her engine room crew in 1905 led to damage which took months to repair, and in 1911 she was struck by lightning, splintering her mast and knocking her radio out of commission. She began to develop a reputation.

During the Edwardian era Britain's transatlantic passenger lines came under threat from the Germans,

Below: The stately Cunard liners *Lusitania* (shown here) and *Mauretania* dominated the Transatlantic run between Southampton and New York during the years before World War I.

CUNARD

Above: The wreck of the German U-boat *U20* off the Danish coast. The *U20* was said to be the submarine that torpedoed the *Lusitania*.

who built a string of modern and fast passenger liners between 1895 and 1905. Of equal importance, American financier J.P. Morgan bought a controlling share in the prestigious White Star Line, as well as in several German and American transatlantic shipping companies. This meant that both Germany and America could also rely on a ready-made fleet of powerful and fast auxiliary warships in time of war. Seen as something of a blow to national pride, the government offered the Cunard Line a loan of £2.6 million to build two new passenger liners which would re-establish Britain's pre-eminence in the transatlantic

Above: The grace of the Edwardian liners (such as the RMS *Lusitania* shown here) gave them an aura of invincibility. But, most sank at sea before they reached the breaker's yard.

Below: A rare photograph of the RMS *Titanic* underway, taken during her calamitous maiden voyage in April 1912.

market. The only proviso was that the ships and the company would remain solely in British hands for 20 years, and that both vessels could be requisitioned in the event of a war and used as the Admiralty saw fit. In addition the government would pay Cunard a £75,000 no-strings subsidy if they agreed. Naturally Cunard's Board jumped at the chance.

The result was the construction of the sister ships RMS *Lusitania* and RMS *Mauretania*. Both vessels were 790 feet (241 m) long, and 88 feet (26 m) across the beam; these steel giants displaced 31,938 tons unladen, had a top speed of 25 knots—making them two of the fastest passenger ships of their day. The *Lusitania* was built on the Clyde in Scotland, while the *Mauretania* was constructed on the Tyne, in north-east England. On her maiden voyage from Liverpool to New York in September 1907 the *Lusitania* set a new transatlantic record, which was duly beaten by the *Mauretania* a few months later. The two well-matched liners continued to

compete for the coveted Blue Ribbon Trophy for the fastest transatlantic crossing, and in the process they left the competition behind.

Then a new rival appeared on the scene. The White Star Line, reluctant to allow Cunard to steal all the glory, approved the construction of three new liners which were intended to outperform the new Cunard vessels. The result was the construction of the *Titanic*, the *Olympic*, and the *Britannic*. The *Olympic* and the *Titanic* were the latest word in opulence: at 853 feet (260 m) long with a beam of 92 feet (28 m), and a displacement of 46,329 tons, they were both considerably larger than her rivals. The *Olympic* was the first of the two to enter service, and for her maiden voyage she was commanded by the same Captain Smith who would later command the *Titanic*. The voyage went smoothly, though soon after she returned to Britain the *Olympic* collided with the British cruiser HMS *Hawke* which put her out of commission for several months.

Above: The RMS *Titanic* was designed to be "virtually" unsinkable, but her watertight bulkheads did not stretch the full height of the ship. When one section was filled, the water tipped over the bulkhead into the next compartment astern, slowly dragging the ship under in the process.

As for the *Titanic*, she was launched in late May 1911, and by March she was delivered to Southampton ready for her maiden voyage. Enough is known about what happened next to permit brevity in this account. Captain Smith sailed from Southampton on April 10, 1912, and late in the evening of April 14, she struck an iceberg in the North Atlantic which gashed her hull and flooded six of her watertight compartments. She was designed to be able to float with four flooded, but not six. It took just over two hours for the liner to sink; before she broke in two, between the third and fourth funnels, her bow sank quickly while her stern slowly rose out of the water, then slipped beneath the waves. Over 1,500 lives were lost in the tragedy, largely because there were insufficient lifeboats to hold all the passengers.

The unlucky *Oceanic* was in Southampton on April 10, when the *Titanic* sailed on her maiden voyage; she was pulled from the quay by the suction, and both the *Oceanic* and the *New York* almost collided. *Oceanic* sailed

Above: When the RMS *Titanic* left Southampton in April 1912, several passengers reportedly preferred to remain behind after experiencing dream-like premonitions of a possible disaster.

several days later, the first liner to leave Britain after news of the *Titanic* disaster had broken. This seemed a bad omen, made worse when a few days later she rescued a lifeboat from the *Titanic*, containing nothing but three decomposed bodies in it.

The outbreak of World War I in August 1914 ended the heyday of these ocean liners. It also led to the

Left: The largest ocean liner since the *Great Eastern*, the RMS *Oceanic* was widely regarded as the most luxurious ship afloat around the turn of the previous century, and one of the most unlucky. She was continually plagued by a string of accidents and collisions throughout her career.

Above: When news of the *Titanic* disaster spread, numerous cases of kindred feelings between siblings were reported when a relation had died in the tragedy.

loss of several of the most prestigious vessels in the transatlantic fleet. When Great Britain declared war, *Oceanic* was converted to war service. As HMS *Oceanic* she left Southampton on August 25, 1914, sent north to Scapa Flow to join the 10th Cruiser Squadron patrolling a 150-mile (241-km) stretch of sea between Scotland and the Faroe Islands, stopping ships as part of the blockade of German ports. On September 7, she was off Foula to the west of Shetland when, due to a navigational error, she struck a skerry called *Da Shaalds*. She remained hard aground despite the efforts of rescue tugs and on September 11 she was declared a complete loss. A salvage vessel recovered her guns, but on September 29, a huge storm lashed the skerry, and she broke up, a sad end to an unlucky ship.

The *Mauretania* was also requisitioned, but the *Lusitania* remained a civilian ship, albeit one which was almost certainly carrying cargoes of munitions on behalf of the Admiralty, her part-owners. On May 7, 1915, a torpedo from the German U-boat UB-20 struck the *Lusitania* on her port side, causing a major explosion which blew a large hole on her starboard side. Though still a matter for conjecture, it was almost certainly caused by the detonation of munitions in her hold. She sank in less than 20 minutes, claiming the lives of over 1,195 people. Next to go was the *Britannic*, sister ship of *Titanic*, which was nearing completion when the war began. Put into service by the navy as a troop transport on November 21, 1916, she struck a mine off the island of Kea in the Aegean and sank with the loss of 74 men.

By the time the war ended in 1918 only the *Mauretania* remained afloat out of all these once great ships. She was soon crippled by a string of minor engine fires culminating in a major blaze in 1923, which caused sufficient damage to keep her out of service for several months. By the time she was ready for sea again the Wall Street Crash and the resulting Great Depression conspired to rob her of the affluent customers she had been built to serve. During her last years she served as a cruise ship in the Caribbean and the Mediterranean. In late 1934 when Cunard and the White Star Line merged, she returned to Britain for the last time, and two years later she was broken up.

Countless stories of premonitions of some of these disasters can be found. Newspapers reported the tale of four friends who deliberately missed the sailing of the

Titanic after one had a dream which suggested something bad would happen to the ship. The *Southampton Times* ran the story of a lad who refused to sign on as a steward at the last moment, largely because he had a similar dream. A handful of passengers canceled their reservations because of similar experiences. A string of premonition-led cancellations emerged following the loss of the *Lusitania*, although as the ship was traveling through U-boat infested waters during wartime, a reluctance to travel could have been explained by other reasons. It is probably the great dignity and majesty of these ships which encourages people to regard them as something special, and also to attribute qualities such as luck or lack thereof to ships of this type. Whether doomed or not, by the end of World War I the heyday of such ocean juggernauts had passed.

Above: The great liners not only carried the cream of society, but also served as immigrant ships, transporting thousands of Europeans to a new life in America. These became the unsung victims of disasters such as the *Titanic* or the *Mauretania* (above).

Left: The RMS *Mauretania* was one of the few great transatlantic liners to survive World War I, but the economic effects of the Wall Street Crash and the Great Depression put paid to the glorious heyday of the transatlantic liners. The often dismal or tragic end to these stately vessels gives them a distinct air of pathos, and encourages their association with supernatural events.

LOSS UNEXPLAINED:
UNSOLVED NAVAL DISASTERS

While the loss of luxurious ocean liners can influence national prestige, the same is also true when major warships are lost, and the disaster can also threaten the security of the owning nation. This is particularly true in time of war or impending conflict: exactly the circumstances in which the three disasters which follow took place. The reason why each of the three battleships blew up without warning has never been satisfactorily explained, although in the case of the USS *Maine* a war-hungry press and public were convinced that Spanish agents were responsible even before a Board of Inquiry had been able to examine the evidence! As a result America declared war on Spain, which turned out to be one of the most one-sided conflicts in modern history.

Naval disasters are not restricted to times of war. The design of sailing warships remained somewhat static for centuries, but with the advent of the ironclad warship, naval designers tried a variety of combinations of hull shapes and weapon types before settling on the design which was most practical. For instance, the Russians built two circular battleships for use on the Black Sea, the idea being they would be highly maneuverable. Instead, they had the seagoing qualities of floating barrels. One of the most famous ironclad warships was the USS *Monitor*, whose engagement with

Left: The CSS *Virginia* doing battle with the USS *Monitor* in the Battle of Hampton Roads, May 9, 1862. The engagement ushered in a new era in naval history. From that point on, warships would be constructed from metal rather than wood.

the CSS *Virginia* off Hampton Roads in 1862 ushered in a new era in naval warfare. Her designer John Ericsson gave her a very low freeboard, so that with her gun turret in place she looked like "a cheesebox on a raft." While this low freeboard made her difficult to hit, it also meant that she was vulnerable in heavy seas. Sure enough, just before 1862 drew to a close the USS *Monitor* foundered in heavy seas off Cape Hatteras. The best element of Ericsson's design was his gun turret, and

in 1867 the Royal Navy commissioned an experimental turret-armed warship, HMS *Captain*. With only six feet (1.8 m) between her upper deck and the waterline she was vulnerable in heavy seas as the *Monitor* had been, with the added danger that the *Captain* was fitted with three conventional sailing masts, which made her top-heavy. Shortly after midnight on September 7, 1870, she capsized during a storm in the Bay of Biscay, and all but 18 of her 499-man crew went down with her.

Below: The USS *Monitor* became the namesake for a whole new class of vessel. Civil War "monitors" such as the USS *Onondaga* (pictured here) had a dangerously low freeboard, which made them unsuitable for operations on the high seas.

These disasters can be blamed on bad ship design, but the loss of HMS *Victoria* was due to nothing more than incompetence. In 1893 the six-year old battleship was the flagship of Vice-Admiral Sir George Tyron, commander of the British Mediterranean Fleet. During a fleet exercise held off Malta on June 22, 1893, Tyron deployed his battle fleet of ten capital ships so they were steaming in two parallel lines, 1,200 yards (1097 m) apart. He planned to close the gap between the two columns to just 400 yards (366 m) by ordering each ship to turn in succession toward the other column. His flag officer suggested there wasn't enough room for the maneuver, but Tyron was adamant. At 3 pm he gave the order, and simultaneously the *Victoria* and the other leading ship HMS *Camperdown* turned toward each other. As the turning circle of both ships was around 800 yards (732 m), the result was inevitable. The two battleships collided; the steel ram fitted to the bow of *Camperdown* sliced into the *Victoria's* hull below the waterline, tearing a 100-foot (30 m) gash in her side. The flagship took 13 minutes to sink, and 357 men were lost in the tragedy. Vice-Admiral Tyron went down with his ship. The only mystery surrounding the disaster was why Tyron had refused to countermand his obviously flawed orders, and why the other officers on the bridges of both ships didn't take matters into their own hands. Traditional British reserve and blind obedience to superiors may have been as much to blame as the incompetence of the fleet commander.

However, these were peacetime disasters and would have taken on a more serious aspect if the country was

Above: The USS *Maine* was raised in 1912 to investigate the cause of her loss. This time it was suggested that the explosion was accidental rather than premeditated.

at war. When the American battleship USS *Maine* entered Havana harbor on a goodwill mission on January 24, 1898, diplomatic tensions between America and Spain were running high. Much of Cuba was in revolt against their Spanish masters, and the press and public in the United States sided with the rebels. The presence of the battleship in Havana was meant to help diffuse the situation and protect American interests, but instead she made matters far worse.

The USS *Maine* was one of the first major warships built for the US Navy after the end of the Civil

War. She took over nine years to complete, so that by the time she entered service in 1895 she had already been overtaken by more modern battleship designs. Nevertheless, although redesignated a second-class battleship, she was still a powerful addition to the American fleet. Displacing 6,682 tons, she was 919 feet (97 m) long, with a beam of 57 feet (17 m). Armed with four ten-inch (25-cm) guns as well as a secondary battery, she was more powerful than any warship in the Spanish fleet, and a floating symbol of America's growing maritime prestige.

On the evening of February 15, 1898, she lay at anchor in Havana harbor, where she could lend aid to the American community in the city if they were threatened by the conflict between Spain and the Cuban insurgents. At 9:10 pm Captain Charles Sigsbee was in his cabin near the stern of the warship, busy writing a letter to his wife. As he wrote he listened to the ship's bugler playing "taps" as the flag was lowered for the night. He later recorded what happened next: "I was enclosing my letter in its envelope when the explosion came. It was a bursting, rending, and crashing roar of immense volume, largely metallic in character. It was followed by heavy, ominous metallic sounds. There was a trembling and lurching motion of the vessel, a list to port. The electric lights went out. Then there was

Left: The baseball team of the USS *Maine*, pictured in Key West just before the battleship sailed for Havana in Cuba. Everyone was killed in the explosion that ripped the warship apart, except for one player.

intense blackness and smoke. The situation could not be mistaken. The *Maine* was blown up and sinking. For a moment the instinct of self-preservation took charge of me, but this was immediately dominated by the habit of command. Crews from nearby ships manned lifeboats to rescue the surviving crewmen of the *Maine*. Chief among them, were the boats from the *Alfonso XII*. The Spanish officers and crews did all that humanity and gallantry could compass."

The ship had blown up near the bow, and everything in front of the forward funnel was a twisted mass of burning metal. The survivors abandoned ship, including a reluctant Captain Sigsbee, who watched his ship burn throughout the night.

At least 254 American sailors and marines were killed in the explosion, with another 59 wounded, of which eight would die over the coming weeks. It was an unprecedented disaster, set firmly in the annals in American naval history, and one that could not be easily explained. The US Navy conducted an inquiry in Key West, but no firm conclusions could be readily found. Sigsbee, his officers, and the other leading survivors from his crew were all questioned, but no hint of negligence could be determined. The possibility that the explosion was an internal one caused by an exploding magazine was largely discounted, which left only one other conclusion. Eventually the Board of Inquiry

Right: The USS *Maine* entering Havana Harbor on January 25, 1898. Three weeks later she was destroyed by an explosion, the cause of which has still not been conclusively explained.

decided that for lack of other evidence, the USS *Maine* had probably been sunk by a mine placed under the bows of the ship. When the mine detonated it exploded the forward magazines. Although no foreign power was singled out for official blame, the public, the press, and even the US government knew exactly who they thought was responsible. Newspaper magnate William Randolph Hearst's *New York Journal* blamed the Spanish, and even printed diagrams showing how Spanish saboteurs had detonated the mine from the shore. War fever mounted, and to encourage circulation men like Hearst and Joseph Pulitzer manufactured stories of Spanish atrocities or complicity in the sinking. This was "yellow journalism" at its most potent. When Frederic Remington arrived in Cuba as an artist working for the *New York Journal*, he cabled Hearst, telling him: "There is no war." Hearst immediately sent a cable back which read: "You furnish the pictures, I'll furnish the war." Hearst was true to his word. After whipping the nation into a frenzy under the rallying cry of "Remember the *Maine*," Hearst got his war. Congress bowed to the pressure, and on April 25, 1898, the country declared war on Spain. Within three months the Spanish were driven out of Cuba, and then the Philippines and Puerto Rico too: the United States had become a true world power.

A second investigation was undertaken 14 years later, and the results were equally inconclusive, although the possibility that the explosion was an internal one was aired for the first time. In the century following the disaster, the arguments over the cause being an

Above and Right: The USS *Maine*—after she was sunk, only her mainmast remained above the water to mark her resting place in the shallow waters of Havana Harbor.

accidental internal explosion or an external force still continued to rage. Due to the overwhelming desire of America to go to war over the incident in the first place, the true facts may never be known.

During World War I two similar disasters resulted in the loss of two Royal Naval battleships. Once again, the argument whether the explosions were caused by saboteurs or by an unfortunate accident has never been properly resolved.

When Britain declared war on Germany on August 4, 1914, the British Grand Fleet moved to its base in Scapa Flow in Orkney, where it was well placed to react to any move made by the German High Seas Fleet based in Kiel. In effect, Britain was mounting a distant blockade of Germany; a cordon of warships which would eventually play a major part in bringing Germany to her knees.

A few years earlier, in 1906 the revolutionary HMS *Dreadnought* entered service. The less well armed and armored warships, which were the mainstay of the fleet, became virtually obsolete. A naval arms race began, with both Britain and Germany competing to build a powerful fleet of dreadnought warships. Although Britain won the race, the hostility created by this competition was a contributory factor to the outbreak of war. As the dreadnought battlefleet went to Scapa Flow in 1914, many of the older "pre-dreadnought" battleships remained in the traditional naval bases of Chatham, Portsmouth, and Plymouth, where they could react to any threat developing from German-occupied Belgium and Northern France.

One of the old "pre-dreadnought" battleships swinging at anchor off Chatham during late 1914 was HMS *Bulwark*, a London Class battleship which had entered service in 1902. Her guns were powerful enough; like most pre-dreadnoughts she carried four main guns, in two turrets. By comparison HMS *Dreadnought* carried ten guns, in five turrets. The more modern ship was also better armored, faster, and had a longer operating range. Still, *Bulwark*'s guns could pound German-held ports quite effectively, or protect the coast from an attack by a hastily-built invasion fleet.

At 7:53 am on November 26, her crew were having breakfast, entertained by the ship's band playing on her quarterdeck. She was moored in a line of warships in Kethole Reach in the River Mersey, with two other large battleships on either side of her: an impressive sight to anyone looking from the shore. The names of the ships of the 5th Battle Squadron had an equally impressive ring: *Bulwark*, *Implacable*, *Irresistible*, *Formidable*, and *Venerable*: nobody names their ships as well as the British.

U.S. AMERICA.   MAINE.

Then, with no warning whatsoever, *Bulwark* blew up. A sheet of flame rose above her masthead, followed by a cloud of dense black smoke, and the sound of a colossal explosion, which was reportedly heard in Whitstable, some 15 miles (24 km) away. Midshipman Charles Drage on board HMS *London* recalled what he saw next: "Such debris as was in the air consisted of small objects and appeared to be largely composed of wood stored on the booms. There were two distinct explosions, and the debris began to fall on our port quarter, a strong wind blowing it away from us. The place where the *Bulwark* had laid was entirely covered with smoke and it was impossible to ascertain the nature, extent or cause of the damage." When the smoke cleared he made out the buoy the battleship had been tied to, and nothing else except for the mast of the battleship protruding from the water, surrounded by debris. Only 12 men survived the disaster, out of a full complement of 714.

An hour later a lookout spotted what he thought was a periscope in the river, suggesting that a U-boat was responsible. Despite sealing off the river with booms, no U-boat was ever found, and no German commander claimed responsibility for the attack. At the inquiry held the following day, most senior officers suggested the disaster was the result of an internal magazine explosion. The court agreed. This didn't stop speculation that the warship had been sabotaged, and incendiary devices with time-delay fuses were known to have been issued for use by German agents before the war began. The strength of these rumors intensified after the minelayer *Princess Irene* blew up near the same anchorage in May 1915. Her decks were laden with high-explosive mines at the time, but this didn't stop the rumors that German agents were responsible for both disasters. Seven months later the armored cruiser HMS *Natal* exploded while at anchor in the Cromarty Firth in

Left: The British pre-dreadnought battleship HMS *Bulwark* was already obsolete when World War I began in August 1914, but she still remained a useful symbol of British naval superiority. Like the USS *Maine* she was ripped apart by an explosion while at anchor on November 26, 1914.

north-east Scotland. Inferior and unstable cordite in her shells was blamed for the accident.

Far more serious was the loss of the modern St. Vincent Class dreadnought battleship HMS *Vanguard* while she lay at anchor in Scapa Flow on the evening of July 9, 1917. A veteran of the Battle of Jutland (1916), *Vanguard* was a modern 19,560-ton battleship, completed in 1910 and a major element of the British High Seas Fleet. Her loss did more to harm British naval supremacy that the loss of all the earlier ships combined. Signalman Charles Mynott serving on HMS *Marlborough* recalled what happened: "I was on watch between 8 pm and midnight and was facing HMS *Vanguard* and saw her start to explode, first aft, two amidships, three foc'sle, and then one huge explosion."

In the explosion 843 sailors died, and of the three survivors, one later died on board the hospital ship.

Once more the cause for the explosion was believed to be a detonation in one of the two munition magazines which served the amidships turrets. Although no finite cause for the cordite explosion was established, the most likely explanation was that a fire in a coal bunker raged undetected long enough to heat the cordite stored in the next compartment, triggering the explosion. It was equally possible that the cordite was also unstable.

Of course, another possibility was sabotage, although nobody ever claimed responsibility. A link was later established with a Chatham dockyard ordnance fitter, who had been on board all four ships during the previous three years, but like so many events in wartime, that was probably just a coincidence. A far more likely cause was that the British were simply using poor-quality cordite, which became unstable with age, and where any significant rise in temperature could lead to disaster.

Left: HMS *Vanguard* was a powerful and modern dreadnought battleship of the St. Vincent Class, and supposedly her design precluded accidents such as those which might have caused the loss of the USS *Maine* and HMS *Bulwark*. Nevertheless she too was destroyed by an explosion while at anchor on July 9, 1917.

STILL ON PATROL:
LOST SUBMARINES

Submarines are significantly more prone to accidents than conventional surface warships, as the additional plane of operation provides far more scope for things to go wrong. Old submariners quip that the secret of their trade is to make sure the number of times they come to the surface is the same as the number of times they dive. By making light of this they make light of the risks involved. During wartime these risks are much greater. For example, during World War II the German Kriegsmarine commissioned over 600 U-boats. By the end of the war less than one in ten remained. The rest were what submariners euphemistically describe as being "still on patrol": missing in action,

almost inevitably through depth charging, enemy torpedoes, air attacks, or diving accidents. The sheer terror of a boat and its crew unable to reach the surface again, or sinking until it reached its "crush depth" where the hull implodes, is so horrifying as to be almost unimaginable. However, this hasn't stopped thousands of brave men of many nationalities venturing out to sea in these frail craft over the past century, and placing their lives in the hands of their fellow crewmen.

One of the strangest submarine losses was World War I German coastal submarine UB-65. She was built at the Vulcan Werft shipyard in Hamburg during late 1916, one of a class of 24 similar vessels of the UBIII

Right: In 1906, Germany first designed the submarine known as the U-boat. Despite heavy casualties, U-boats proved to be one of the most effective weapons in the German arsenal.

Class, six of which were built in the Hamburg yard. She was launched in June 1917, and was attached to the 2nd U-boat Flotilla based at Bruges in Belgium. Like her sister boats she was a powerful craft, just over 60 yards (55 m) long, displacing 516 tons on the surface, and armed with ten 20-inch (50-cm) torpedoes and a 3.4-inch (88-mm) deck gun. Designated a coastal submarine, her role was to maintain a submarine blockade of Britain; her diesel engines gave her a range of 8,500 miles (13,680 km) on the surface, and a maximum surface speed of 13 knots. Conditions were very spartan for the 34-men crew, the sailors having to "hot bunk" with one man sleeping while another allocated the same bunk was on watch. For officers, it wasn't much better.

UB-65 developed a reputation as an unlucky ship long before she entered service. During her construction two dockyard workers were crushed to death in an accident while laying her keel, and later three more engineers were killed by asphyxiation in her engine room when her batteries leaked sulfuric acid fumes into the enclosed space. Soon after the boat arrived in Bruges she left on her first active patrol, only to have a petty-officer washed overboard and drowned. Her first operational dive proved a disaster as her buoyancy tanks failed, and it took 12 hours for her oxygen-starved crew to bring her to the surface. Worse, her batteries had started leaking again while she was submerged, and several of her crew were temporarily overcome by the fumes. Her next accident took place in port, when one of her torpedoes detonated by accident, killing the five men on duty in her forward torpedo room, including her second officer.

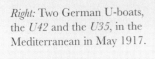

Right: Two German U-boats, the *U42* and the *U35*, in the Mediterranean in May 1917.

It took four months to repair the damage in an Antwerp dry dock, but by December 1917 she was ready for action again. When her crew reported for duty the story of the doomed submarine became even more bizarre. A terrified sailor on harbor watch reported that he had seen the boat's former second officer walk onto the ship during the night. For the next few months the ghost was sighted several more times, sometimes standing on the conning tower when the boat was on the surface, or else standing on the foredeck above the torpedo room. A week later the commanding officer was killed in an air attack on the port. Morale plummeted, and many of UB-65's crew demanded transfers. When these were denied, some deserted, preferring to face a firing squad than a ghost. According to German sources, one sailor who deserted later testified that: "UB-65 was never a happy ship, though we were always fortunate with our officers ... I am convinced myself she was haunted. One night at sea I saw an officer standing on deck ... a shipmate who was nearer swore that he recognized our former second officer, who had been killed long before by a torpedo explosion. On other nights, while lying in my bunk, I saw a strange officer walk through the ship. He always went to the forward torpedo room, but never came out again."

In May 1918 a sailor who encountered the ghost was so terrified that he had to be sedated. The following day he jumped overboard and was drowned. Another sailor was lost overboard a few days later, bringing the death toll up to nine sailors and five civilians. The seemingly fated submarine apparently met her end just off Cape Clear in Southern Ireland on July 10, 1918. She was sighted on the surface by the US Navy submarine L-2. The American boat prepared to fire two torpedoes, but before she could turn into position the German submarine exploded and sank. The reason for her loss remains a mystery, but the likely explanations were that either she tried to fire a torpedo at the American boat but it detonated in the torpedo room, sinking the boat, or even that another German submarine, the UB-62 which was in the same area fired on her by mistake. The story persists that the last thing the American skipper saw before she sank was the sight

Right: Submarines are vulnerable to accidents, which is why many losses are never fully explained. The wrecks of at least 16 British submarines, similar to this one, lie in the English Channel.

of a German officer nonchalantly standing on the conning tower, his arms folded. Unfortunately this was never mentioned in any report, nor was any truth found in the tale that L-2 had to be dry-docked due to the buckling of her plates caused by the explosion of UB-65. One final twist to the tale is the recent discovery of a German Type UBIII U-boat on the seabed six miles (10 km) off the Cornish fishing village of Padstow. An identity plate fitted by one of her two propellers is supposed to identify her as UB-65, which is highly unlikely, as the U-boat was supposed to have been sunk off Southern Ireland. Clearly more investigative work

needs to be done to figure out where exactly the boat went down, and why. What is clear is that, haunted or not, the crew of UB-65 regarded her as a doomed ship, and she did eventually sink in mysterious circumstances with all hands.

The wrecks of at least 16 British submarines lie in the waters of the English Channel, and the exact cause of many of the losses have never been satisfactory explained. One of these boats is HMS *Affray*. Launched in late 1945, the A-Class boat embodied all the design and construction lessons learned during World War II, and consequently she was seen as the latest word in

submarines. Not only was she well appointed with relatively spacious crew quarters and air conditioning plants, she was also the best-armed boat in the fleet, with no less than ten torpedo tubes. On April 16, 1951, she disappeared while on a training exercise in the Channel. By the following morning a full-scale search had got underway, but despite the deployment of dozens of ships and aircraft it took a full three months to locate her. The air inside her hull would have run out after three days, so there was no longer any hope of saving the 75 men trapped inside her. Speculation had run rife, with stories of Soviet agents or submarines, unexploded wartime mines, and even rogue German submarines all making the rounds. One story even suggested she had been spirited off to Russia. She was finally located on June 14, lying in 278 feet (88 m) of water off Portland Bill. Her hull was still intact, and her periscope extended, with her planes set at a steep ascent angle.

There was no sign that anyone had tried to escape from her hull after she settled, suggesting some catastrophic disaster had overwhelmed the boat before her crew could react. It was then found that her snorkel mast had snapped off, or failed, which would have let water flood into her hull. While this could have caused the disaster, it was equally likely that an internal battery explosion had caused the boat to flood. Either way she would have filled with water within minutes and sunk to the seabed. Divers have recently relocated the wreck, and so the likelihood is that new evidence might well emerge which could help explain the mysterious loss of HMS *Affray*.

Equally baffling is the loss of the American submarine R-12. The 569-ton submarine was built in 1919, and by the time the United States entered the war in 1941 she was considered obsolete. During the 1930s she had been mothballed, but she was hurriedly re-activated and used as a stopgap until more modern

Left: The post-war British submarine HMS *Affray* was one of the most modern diesel boats in the British fleet when she went down in the English Channel with all hands on April 16, 1951.

boats could enter service. By 1943 she had been relegated to a support role, and together with other R-boats she was attached to the Submarine and Sonar Testing School based in Key West, Florida. While surface ships practiced sonar detection on the boats, the submarines were used to train recruits in the intricacies of submarine warfare.

On June 12, 1943, she slipped out of Key West and after clearing the coral reef she headed south-east to conduct torpedo drills. Shortly after noon she prepared to dive when suddenly she began to flood by the bow. The alarm was sounded and the skipper gave orders to close the hatches and blow the main ballast, but the control room was flooded before the boat could be saved.

She sank within 15 seconds, taking 42 men down with her. The only survivors were the bridge crew, who were able to jump clear before they were sucked under. The cause of the disaster remains unclear, but the likelihood is that one of her torpedo tubes was opened by mistake, while the forward bow cap (the seaward end of the torpedo tube) was also opened. In these circumstances a column of water would jet through the two-foot (61-cm) diameter opening with such a force that the boat would flood before anyone had a chance to react.

This clearly demonstrates how vulnerable submarines are, compared to surface vessels, and why so many submarine losses have never been satisfactorily explained. With no overtly visible evidence to go by, it is easy to turn a commonplace accident or tragic disaster into something much more mysterious, and to blame the events on something other than mechanical or human error.

Left: The pre-war submarine *R-12* was one of the oldest boats in the US Navy when she was lost off Key West on June 12, 1943. The only survivors were the men of her bridge party, who were left on the surface as their boat sank beneath them.

THE SUPERNATURAL AT SEA

We have already ascertained that sailors have a tradition of being superstitious. They know just how humbling the sheer scale of the ocean can be, and how fickle. For as long as man has gone to sea there have been ghost stories associated with ships, from those encountered by Odysseus in the pages of Homer's *Odyssey* to those supposedly encountered by tourists on board the liner *Queen Mary*. There is the well-documented case of the haunting of the World War I submarine UB-65, and the story of the Flying Dutchman, whose ship has been seen by German submariners two generations later. Even more alarming than ghosts who appear on board a ship are the cases when the ship itself is the ghost, reportedly sailing on for eternity, doomed to recreate the tragedy which resulted in its loss. The following selection of accounts of haunted vessels and phantom ships have been selected to give a cross section of these tales, rather than form a complete catalogue of them. After all, there are probably too many such tales to include in a book ten times the size of this. Instead the following serve to encourage the questioning of tales of this kind, and to seek out ways these incidents can be explained. I have offered as many logical explanations as I can. In some cases, no such solution seems apparent. Feel free to make up your own mind whether the following accounts represent just strange coincidences, hoaxes, delusions or if they really do represent a manifestation of another spiritual or supernatural plane.

Above: The cocktail lounge on board the SS *Queen Mary*. The liner has been associated with several ghosts during her long career.

HAUNTED SHIPS
THE SS *GREAT EASTERN* (1858)

She was a ship ahead of her time, the largest, most technologically advanced steamship ever built. Isambard Kingdom Brunel's *Great Eastern* seemed to defy the laws of engineering, a floating testimony to the industrial age and the ascent of man over nature. As the leading engineer of his age, Brunel was used to challenges; but for him the idea that a steamship could travel from Australia to Europe without taking on board more coal was a maritime "Holy Grail." Brunel began working on plans for a steamship of biblical proportions, and the result was one which his shipbuilding partner John Scott Russell described as "a museum of inventions." Despite reservations, Russell undertook the building of Brunel's masterpiece at his yard at Millwall,

Below: The grand salon of the SS *Great Eastern* depicted during a violent storm. It was this room which was ripped apart by the explosion caused by a pressure build-up in her funnel casings during her maiden voyage in 1859.

Above: The imposing appearance of the SS *Great Eastern* made her an attractive image of transatlantic glamour and commerce, but she also had a more sinister reputation.

on the Thames just below London. Brunel's vessel would be 700 feet (210 m) long, with a beam of 83 feet (25 m), which made her larger than any vessel in history. It would be another four decades before a steamship of comparable size would put to sea. To give the vessel strength she was reinforced by a unique system of frames, and her hull protected by a revolutionary double bottom. Brunel even included watertight compartments into her design. She was powered by paddlewheels on both sides and a single screw, though she could also rely on sails. The six-masted, four-funneled colossus was

launched in January 1858; by September the following year her fitting-out was complete, and she was ready for her sea trials. That was when the trouble first began.

On September 5, 1859 the *Great Eastern*'s Captain Harrison steered his new vessel down the Thames on her trial voyage, bound for Weymouth. If all went well she would sail for Holyhead in Anglesey, where she would take on passengers for her maiden voyage to New York. All she carried that day were anxious owners and engineers, and carefree guests. All seemed to be going well as the steamship passed Dover and headed west up the English Channel. Although the ship boasted a sumptuous grand saloon, most of the guests preferred to remain on the upper deck, where they were able to watch the coastline pass by. However, below deck, everything was far from well. Brunel's design called for a water-filled iron cooling jacket to be fitted to the base of each of the four funnels, and when this water reached boiling point it was vented out through steam pipes running up each funnel. In order to test the efficiency of the system stopcocks had been fitted to each steam vent, but for some reason the ones associated with the two central funnels had not been removed. These were the funnels which passed up through the main saloon to the upper deck, their utilitarian surface screened behind boxes of mirrored glass which stretched the full height of the saloon. When the ship sailed, the stopcocks had been checked, and were open. Around the time the ship steamed passed Dover, they mysteriously closed again, even though they were sealed in specially constructed housings. Everyone remained oblivious to the potential

Above: Isambard Kingdom Brunel saw the SS *Great Eastern* as his crowning achievement, but he died ten days before her maiden voyage.

blew into the air, showering debris onto the upper deck. Down in the engine room the blast killed six stokers, who were scalded to death by the spray of boiling water. An astute engineering officer realized what had happened, and ordered the second stopcock to be checked. The box securing it was unlocked and the stopcock was found to be closed. The engineer opened it, and a shrieking cloud of steam erupted from the funnel. A second explosion had been averted with minutes to spare.

The obvious explanation for the tragedy was that someone had left the stopcocks closed. However, during the inquiry which followed it transpired that an officer and two engineers had checked the valves before the ship sailed, and assured the court that they had been left open when the boxes covering them were locked shut. The keys were kept in the engine room, and access was restricted. While sabotage was considered, there was no real motive, and nobody came forward to claim responsibility. Therefore the explosion remains somewhat mysterious, and to this day no satisfactory examination has been found. However, this turned out to be only the first of many tragedies and accidents to occur on the *Great Eastern* during the next 30 years, causing the deaths of, on average, one person each year. Crewmen were killed when fittings or machinery broke loose without warning, or passengers and crew were lost overboard. Several fatal fires broke out in the engine room and cabins, while several dockside fires broke out when she was in port in Liverpool or New York. She also collided with several smaller vessels in both ports,

catastrophe, and the pressure built up steadily until 6 pm, when the cooling jacket of the second funnel exploded. The funnel burst, sending fragments of metal from the funnel and glass from the mirrors the length of the saloon, which then filled with a spray of steam and boiling water. Fortunately the saloon was empty, save for the Captain Harrison's daughter, who was protected from the blast by a metal bulkhead. The funnel itself sinking or badly damaging them in the process. She certainly seemed to be an unlucky ship, and people began to wonder how all these fatalities and accidents might be connected.

The more superstitious mariners pointed out that the vessel's initial launch had been a fiasco, due to the technical problems of moving such a large vessel from the slipyard into the River Thames. Consequently it was delayed for several weeks. That in itself was meant to be unlucky. Another even more widely held superstition was that the ship was haunted. Sailors and passengers both complained of hearing hammering noises from outside the hull. Even Captain Harrison complained of the noise. Both he and the Chief Engineer suspected

that something had broken loose between the outer and inner hulls. In June 1862 the *Great Eastern* struck a rock while entering New York Harbor, causing an 80-foot (24-m) gash in her hull. As no dry dock was large enough to accommodate her, a caisson was built around the gash, allowing workers access to the lower hull. After a week the men downed tools, complaining that they had clearly heard the sound of hammering coming from the space between the two hulls. To allay their fears the ship's new commander, Captain Evans, ordered a complete inspection of the lower hull, which found a broken swivelling joint on the underside of the port paddlewheel, which regularly struck against the hull to make a hammering sound. Their fears allayed, the

Below: The aftermath of the mysterious explosion which destroyed the grand salon of the SS *Great Eastern* during her maiden voyage. The remains of her damaged funnel lie strewn across her upper deck.

engineers returned to their work. Unfortunately, when the ship put to sea again, the mysterious hammering began again. After that, rumors that the ship was haunted became even more widespread. When the writer Jules Verne sailed in the *Great Eastern* in 1868 he heard several different versions of the ghost story; one that it was the ghost of an engineer who was scalded to death, another that it was the ghost of a female passenger, and a third—the most persistent version— that it was the ghost of a riveter, who had been accidentally sealed between the two hulls of the ship when she was built. The hammering was attributed to him, signaling to the crew that his soul needed to

escape. A fourth version claimed that two riveters were trapped, the second being the young apprentice of the first.

The SS *Great Eastern* was never the success Brunel had expected it to be, and the calamities which befell his ship only helped to limit its popularity with travelers. She was finally broken up in Birkenhead in the late 1880s, and despite a rumor to the contrary, no skeleton was found inside the hull. While she might not have been haunted, she did prove a highly unlucky ship, and in those circumstances, even the most illogical of explanations are sought to help explain her run of bad luck.

Below: The SS *Great Eastern* approaching harbor in New York. Despite her links with ghosts and the propensity for accidents to occur on board, she remained the most glamorous means of transatlantic travel for two generations.

H M S   *A S P*   (1 8 5 0)

After the Napoleonic Wars ended in 1815, the Royal Navy reduced the size of its sailing battlefleet, paying off or mothballing several veterans of sea battles such as St. Vincent, the Nile, and Trafalgar. The only part of the fleet which continued to grow during the decades which followed was the Survey Fleet: the relatively small vessels used to chart the oceans, conduct scientific experiments and explore unmapped regions of the world.

One of these survey vessels was HMS *Asp*. She began life as the sidewheel steamer *Fury*, built in Harwich during 1823 as a mail packet on behalf of the postal service. The first steamship was built in 1783, and so in 1823 steamships were a relatively new invention; the *Fury* was therefore one of this first commercially viable paddlewheel-driven steamships. For the next eight years the small 120-ton ship plied the English Channel between Dover and Ostend in Belgium until she was replaced by a larger, faster vessel. She then operated the mail link between Portpatrick in south-west Scotland and Donaghadee, near Bangor in Ireland. In 1837 she was officially retired from service, and offered to the Navy. Although they took her into service, renaming her the *Asp* she was retained as the Scotland to Ireland packet for another 11 years, until a suitable replacement could be built. She didn't properly come under naval command until 1848. After a major overhaul in Portsmouth which involved the replacement of her engines and paddlewheels, she began her new career as

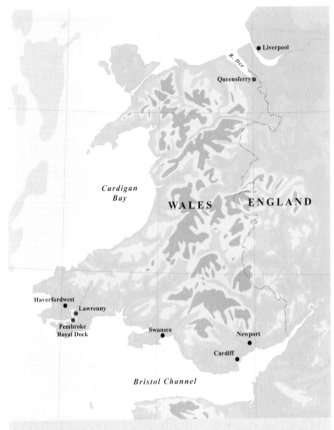

Above: The crew believed the *Asp* was haunted. Ghostly happenings were reported while it was anchored in many locations, including Liverpool and Haverfordwest, Wales.

a naval survey ship. Her first captain was 33-year-old Lieutenant George Alldridge, and the *Asp* was his first command.

When Alldridge arrived in Portsmouth in March 1850 to assume his command, the Superintendent of the Royal Dockyard told him his new ship was haunted. The dockyard workers then refused to work on her for the same reason. Alldridge was skeptical of such superstition, and told the Superintendent as much. The work was eventually completed, but the ghost rumors refused to go away. During her naval life, which spanned three decades, the *Asp* was used to conduct detailed surveys of the approaches to Liverpool, and the waters around the Welsh coast. Her efforts resulted in the first printed Admiralty Charts of the area, and to cap that, she even participated in the laying of the first submarine cable between Wales and Ireland, snaking along the seabed from Holyhead to Dublin. However, for the first seven of these years she seemed to play host to an unwanted passenger.

In late May 1850 Lieutenant Alldridge took the *Asp* to the Dee Estuary near Liverpool, where the ship was due to be used to survey the area. One evening the ship was at anchor in the estuary, and Alldridge was joined in his cabin by the Ship's Master, George MacFarlane. The two men were in the habit of reading aloud to each other, but that evening they were interrupted by noises from the after cabin, separated from their own by a small space housing the companionway running to the upper deck. At first the men thought it was the steward, and MacFarlane called out to him; "Don't make such a noise." The sound stopped, only to start again a minute or so later. Again the officer called out, but the noise continued. The Master rose from the table, picked up a lantern and went to the other cabin. It was empty. Somewhat confused he returned to the table, and the two men continued their reading. The noise began again, sounding like someone moving furniture, then staggering around the after cabin, as if they were drunk. This time both men went to investigate. Once more, the cabin was empty.

Over the next few years the noises were repeated regularly, and still no rational explanation for them could be found. Alldridge later recounted one incident when both he and MacFarlane had been invited ashore to Queensferry on the River Dee, and had returned around 10 pm. On descending the companionway they both heard someone scuttle from one cabin to the other. They thought they'd caught a sailor rifling through the captain's possessions. On entering his cabin, Alldridge gave MacFarlane his sword and whispered to him to stand guard at the companionway. He then opened the door into the far cabin, only to find it completely empty. On other occasions he heard furniture being moved in both cabins, and even the sound of a gun being fired. Often the sounds were also heard by others, including MacFarlane. Alldridge claimed he became used to the sounds, and even in a stiff upper-lipped way that he "had taken some kind of pleasure in listening to the various sounds." In 1854 the *Asp* was lying off the picturesque village of Lawrenny, upriver from Haverfordwest in South Wales. It was a Sunday, and virtually the entire crew were ashore, either in the village church or in the alehouse at Lawrenny Quay. One of the few men to remain on board was the steward. He was descending the companionway leading to the two cabins when he heard a female's voice, smelled her perfume, and heard her brushing her hair, though there was no one there. Stricken with fear, the steward fainted. When Alldridge returned to the ship and encountered his steward he "found his appearance so altered" with fear as to be almost unrecognizable.

After his experience the man begged a discharge, and left the ship.

One evening while the ship was at anchor Alldridge was disturbed in his cabin by the Ship's Quartermaster, who asked him to come on deck, claiming that the lookout had seen something unusual. He certainly had. As Alldridge emerged he saw the figure of a woman standing on the starboard paddle-wheel box, one arm outstretched with a finger pointing skyward. Soon afterward she disappeared. The vision returned on several occasions, each time adopting the same posture. These visitations proved too much for many of the *Asp*'s crew, who regularly pleaded for their discharge papers, and when they were not granted, they deserted. To solve a growing morale problem, Alldridge called in a clergyman, who agreed that "some troubled spirit must be lingering about the vessel." Despite his best efforts, the ghost remained on board.

Below: A small Royal Naval sidewheel sloop of similar appearance to the survey vessel HMS *Asp*. According to her former captain the vessel played host to the ghost of a woman who haunted the ship for several years before she found rest in a dockside graveyard.

The ghostly affair finally reached its climax in November 1857 when the *Asp* put in to Pembroke Royal Dockyard in south-west Wales to have the underside of her hull re-coppered. At the time the dockyard and associated shipyard were guarded by soldiers from the 8th Royal Dockyard Corps. The night the ship arrived, the captain and most of the crew were ashore, and sentries patrolled the dock. During the evening watch (8 pm to midnight) a sentry saw the ghostly figure of a woman standing on her paddlewheel box, pointing a hand at the sky. As he watched the figure moved onto the edge of the dry dock and came toward him. The soldier raised his musket and challenged the woman, demanding: "Who goes there?" The figure paid no heed, and continued on, as if she intended to pass through the man. Understandably the sentry dropped his musket and ran. A second sentry saw the incident, and fired his musket into the air as a signal to call out the dockyard's duty guard. By this time a third soldier arrived on the scene, and watched the woman walk through the open dockyard gate and turn away to the right. The figure approached the 13th century ruins of Pater Church and entered the churchyard. The terrified sentry watched the woman stand over one of the graves, point her finger into the air again, then vanish. According to Alldridge the dockyard sentries were so alarmed by the apparition that the guards were doubled that night. After that the ghost was never seen nor heard from again, and the *Asp* was finally left in peace.

We know so much about the incident because after he retired, Alldridge wrote down the story, and it was published in the *Pembroke Country Guardian* on February 16, 1901. Commander Alldridge was seen as a witness with impeccable credentials, and his account was both lucid and well presented, without a trace of sensationalism. He remained the consummate naval officer, reporting events as he had remembered them. However, he also included his own speculation as to the identity of the ghost. According to Alldridge's account, at some stage shortly before she was finally handed over to the Navy in 1848 the *Fury* arrived in Portpatrick on what was to be her last run as a mail and passenger packet. After the handful of passengers had disembarked a cleaning lady entered the ladies' cabin to find a young woman lying on her bunk with her throat cut. The identity of the woman and the murderer were never found, despite (according to Alldridge) the best efforts of the authorities. Unfortunately, searches through the local papers and the *Scotsman* newspaper of the time have revealed no evidence to support Alldridge's murder story. He listed no source for his claim, so presumably he heard the story second-hand, and the tale may have been misheard or misinterpreted.

Apart from that, the account he gave of the series of ghostly events which took place during his time in command of HMS *Asp* are probably an accurate version of what happened as he remembered it. Perhaps more evidence will one day come to light which will explain what happened; until then, we have to believe in the testimony of a highly respected and experienced Victorian officer and gentleman: who once commanded a haunted ship.

THE YACHT *SPRAY* (1895)

Magellan may have been the first man to attempt a circumnavigation of the globe, but he did so in a well-provisioned ship, with a substantial crew. It was not until the last years of the 19th century that a sailor would undertake the voyage single-handed. Joshua Slocum was one of the most respected sea captains on the American Atlantic coast, with a long and distinguished career at sea. However, on April 24, 1895, the 51-year-old master mariner left Boston in his small specially-adapted sloop *Spray* and sailed around the world, making him the world's first solo circumnavigator of the planet. He returned from his 46,000 mile (73,766 km) voyage just over three years later, on June 27, 1898. After his return he wrote a book describing his experiences, and in 1900 *Sailing alone around the world* became a best-seller. It also revealed that for the space of two days, Slocum believed he was not alone. The Canadian-born sea captain was one of the most famous mariners of his day, and a man regarded for his great integrity. Why then would he claim that during his voyage he had been visited by the ghost of an ancient mariner?

Below: Slocum was an experienced American skipper with a great knowledge of transatlantic conditions. This three-masted vessel, captained by Slocum, is the *Northern Light* bound for Liverpool in 1885 (reproduced from *Century Magazine*, September1889).

DRAWN BY W. TABER.

THE "NORTHERN LIGHT," CAPTAIN JOSHUA SLOCUM, BOUND FOR LIVERPOOL, 1885.

When Joshua Slocum set out on his voyage, he did so in a boat he had virtually rebuilt from scratch. In 1892 his friend Captain Pierce offered him an old boat that "wants some repairs." He found the derelict former Delaware oyster boat propped up in a field outside Fairport, Massachusetts, and the notion of converting her, then sailing her around the world was born. Slocum later recalled that "whaling captains came from far to survey it" as the reconstruction work progressed, and one even conceded that her rebuilt bow was "fit to smash ice." The work took three years, but the end result was that she became a strong, easily-handled vessel, with a gaff-rigged mainmast, and an additional mizzen in her stern. Two rounded cabin structures gave Slocum all the protection he needed from the elements.

After provisioning his small craft and saying farewell to his wife Hattie, he set sail into the Atlantic. He reached the Azores in mid-July, then set a course for Gibraltar on July 24. This is when his account takes a bizarre turn. The American consul in Fayal had presented him with a local cheese, and Slocum also took on board a small sack of plums, both of which he ate during his first night at sea. Within hours he was stricken by food poisoning. Worse, the weather was changing, and a south-westerly gale sprang up. Somehow he managed to haul in his mainsail, and his ship ran with the wind through the heavy seas. At one stage Slocum passed out. What happened next is best told in his own words.

"When I came to, as I thought, from my swoon, I realized that the sloop was plunging into a heavy sea,

Above: Joshua Slocum (1844–1909), the first man to single-handedly circumnavigate the globe.

and looking out of the companionway, to my amazement I saw a tall man at the helm. His rigid hand, grasping the spokes of the wheel, held them as in a vice. One may imagine my astonishment. His rig was that of a foreign sailor, and the large red cap he wore was cockbilled over his left ear, and all was set off with shaggy black whiskers. He would have been taken for a pirate in any part of the world. While I gazed upon his

Above: When Slocum was stricken by food poisoning during a storm, he claimed the ghost of the *Pinta*'s pilot appeared to steer the *Spray* through the tempest. The *Pinta* was the smallest of the three ships which formed Columbus's expedition in 1492.

threatening aspect I forgot the storm, and wondered if he had come to cut my throat. This he seemed to divine. 'Señor,' said he, doffing his cap, 'I have come to do you no harm.' And a smile, the faintest in the world, but still a smile, played on his face, which seemed not unkind when he spoke. 'I have come to do you no harm. I have sailed free,' he said, 'but was never worse than a *contrabandista*. I am one of Columbus's crew,' he continued. 'I am the pilot of the *Pinta* come to aid you. Lie quiet, señor captain,' he added, 'and I will guide your ship tonight. You have a *calentura*, but you will be all right to-morrow.' I thought what a very devil he was to carry sail. Again, as if he read my mind, he exclaimed: 'Yonder is the *Pinta* ahead; we must overtake her. Give her sail; give her sail! *Vale, vale, muy vale!* "

By Slocum's dead reckoning the *Spray* made 90 miles (144 km) that night, and all the time the vessel was kept on course by the ghostly mariner.

Slocum wrote: "I felt grateful to the old pilot, but I marveled some that he had not taken in the jib. The

55

gale was moderating, and by noon the sun was shining. A meridian altitude and the distance on the patent log, which I always kept towing, told me that she had made a true course throughout the 24 hours. I was getting much better now, but was very weak, and did not turn out reefs that day or the night following, although the wind fell light; but I just put my wet clothes out in the sun when it was shining, and, lying down there myself, fell asleep. Then who should visit me again but my old friend of the night before, this time, of course, in a dream. 'You did well last night to take my advice,' said he, 'and if you would, I should like to be with you often on the voyage, for the love of adventure alone.'

"Finishing what he had to say, he again doffed his cap and disappeared as mysteriously as he came, returning, I suppose, to the phantom *Pinta*. I awoke much refreshed, and with the feeling that I had been in the presence of a friend and a seaman of vast experience. I gathered up my clothes, which by this time were dry, then, by inspiration, I threw overboard all the plums in the vessel."

Spray reached Gibraltar a few days later, and an embarrassed Slocum made no mention of encountering the benevolent ghost who saved his life. However, he recalled the story in his best-selling book, a strange action for a sea captain who was otherwise seen as a pillar of rectitude. While his account might easily be dismissed as the fevered ramblings of a sick man, Slocum remained convinced that his ship only managed to ride out a deadly gale which stripped his decks of fittings and bleached them "as white as shark's teeth." If

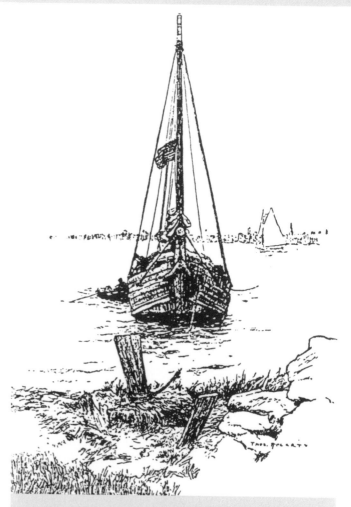

Above: The yacht *Spray* was specially converted by Slocum from the worn-out shell of a fishing boat into a vessel which was perfectly suited for the solo yachtsman.

nothing else, it suggests that not all ghostly apparitions are to be feared, and that even the most hardened mariner can be made to believe in ghosts.

Slocum could have used his ghostly pilot 14 years later. On November 14, 1909, at the age of 65, Slocum set out on another solo voyage, this time bound for the Orinoco River in South America. He sailed from Vineyard Haven on Martha's Vineyard, Massachusetts, and set a south-easterly course into the Atlantic. He was never seen again.

THE SS *ST. PAUL* (1918)

Before we turn from maritime ghosts to the subject of ghostly ships it might be interesting to examine two cases of supposedly haunted liners, both of which have Anglo-American connections. Although both stories are completely different, a common thread can be traced in both cases.

The first concerns the *St. Paul*, a 14,910-ton liner built in Philadelphia, Pennsylvania in 1895. She was owned by the American Line, and used on the route between New York, Southampton, and Cherbourg. Compared to some other liners of the time she was high-sided and rather ungainly, but that was in part because she was a ship with a dual purpose. Congress and the American Line had struck a deal, so that in time of war, she could be chartered by the Navy as either an auxiliary armed cruiser or as a troopship. Her first call to the colors came in 1898, during the Spanish-American War when she was served as an auxiliary cruiser in the West Indies, and was then used to transport troops to Cuba, including Roosevelt's famous "Rough Riders." In September she was handed back to the American Line, who turned her back into a luxury liner. Almost two decades later she would be pressed into service as a troopship again. However, that lay in the future. In 1899 she made maritime history. On November 15, the radio pioneer Gugliemo Marconi on board the *St. Paul* exchanged morse code messages with a transmitter station on the Isle of Wight; the first ever ship to shore communication.

In 1899 she made maritime history. On November 15, the radio pioneer Gugliemo Marconi on board the *St. Paul* exchanged morse code messages with a transmitter station on the Isle of Wight; the first ever ship to shore communication.

Nine years later her fame turned to notoriety. On April 25, 1908, the *St. Paul* left Southampton bound for Cherbourg, and after slipping her tugs she headed out into the Solent. Captain Passow was assisted by a local pilot, George Bowyer, and he needed help, because the wind was rising to gale force, and unseasonable snow showers were forecast. Once in the wider Solent the liner increased speed to 21 knots and changed course to starboard, taking her around the western side of the Isle of Wight into the English Channel. The spit at Hurst Castle reduced the waterway to less than a mile, so the liner reduced speed to 11 knots, a move which coincided with the first snow shower, which reduced visibility to around half a mile (800 m). Then another ship loomed out of the snow. She was the small cruiser HMS

Gladiator, commanded by Captain Lumsden, and with his ship steaming at nine knots, the two ships were closing at alarming speed. Both captains had just over two minutes and 20 seconds before the ships would collide. Lumsden then altered course to port, although international convention dictated ships should both alter to starboard in these circumstances. In this case the narrow channel didn't permit any other move. The *St. Paul* also turned to starboard, meaning that the two ships were still on a collision course. Both captains tried to reverse engines, but it was too late. At 2:38 pm the bow of the *St. Paul* sliced into the starboard quarter of the British cruiser, just above the boiler room. As the liner backed away, water poured into the cruiser, and only the fast thinking of her naval crew prevented the disaster being much worse. They sealed watertight bulkheads to contain the flooding, then Captain Lumsden steered his stricken vessel toward the shore, beaching her in shallow water. Although she lurched over onto her side, enough of the ship remained above water that the survivors had something to clamber on to and wait to be rescued. Twenty-seven sailors died as a result of the accident. The liner limped back to Southampton where her damaged bows were repaired. In the Court of Inquiry which followed, both Captains were held partly responsible; Passow for steaming too fast, and Lumsden for altering course to port.

Ten years later, after the United States entered World War I on the Allied side in April 1917, the SS *St. Paul* was taken over by the Navy once more, who planned to use her as a troopship. The conversion job was designated Project 1643, and the liner taken to

Below: On April 25, 1908, the liner SS *St. Paul* collided with a British warship and sank it. Ten years later, to the hour, the liner herself capsized in New York Harbor.

Brooklyn to be fitted out and repainted in wartime gray. By April 25, the work was complete, and tugs were sent to steer the liner over to Pier 61 on the North River. She lacked her usual ballast, and after the conversion Captain Mills noted she was riding high in the water and listing slightly to port. He ordered her ballast tanks to be filled and the list corrected. As she came alongside the pier the list increased rapidly; her hull slid away from the jetty, snapping the mooring lines which had just been rigged. She continued to heel over until she rested on the bed of the river. Four lives were lost in the seemingly inexplicable accident. Divers examining the hull found that a port used to dump ash from the boiler furnaces had been left open, and the initial list had caused water to pour into the lower boiler room spaces. Although the liner was salvaged some months later and returned to the American Line, they decided not to repair her, and the vessel was scrapped in Wilhelmshaven in 1923.

Despite investigations for both negligence and sabotage, no reasons could be found to explain why the ash hatch had been opened. Inevitably, someone suggested ghosts were involved, and this led to an examination of the liner's history. It was soon pointed out that the *St. Paul* sank at 2.30 pm on April 25, 1918. That was exactly ten years almost to the minute since she sank the *Gladiator*. For many, the coincidence was just too great. Had the ghost of one of the British sailors returned to the *St. Paul* ten years after his death, to wreak vengeance on the American liner? Was it just an incredible coincidence; two maritime tragedies linked only by the same liner?

Left: HMS *Gladiator* was a protected cruiser of the Arrogant Class, identical to her sister ship HMS *Arrogant* (pictured here). The British warship sank in shallow water within minutes of being rammed by the *St. Paul.*

SS QUEEN MARY (1934)

Another ocean-going liner with a ghostly past is none other than the elegant and venerable SS *Queen Mary*, owned by the Cunard Line. Launched on the River Clyde in Scotland in 1934, the luxurious 80,774-ton ship began her maiden voyage on the Southampton, Cherbourg, and New York route on May 27, 1936. She soon developed a reputation as the fastest ocean liner afloat, and became the frequent holder of the coveted Blue Ribbon Trophy for the fastest transatlantic crossing. During World War II she was used as a troopship, and was known as the "Gray Ghost" because of her gray wartime paint and for her ability to slip through U-boat infested waters so quickly that the German submariners were unable to catch her. When the United States entered the fight in December 1941 she began ferrying GIs to Europe, and by the end of the conflict she had transported over a million troops across the Atlantic, as well as from Australia to Europe. She was finally withdrawn from service in 1967, and she is now berthed in Long Beach, California, where she has become a floating hotel and tourist attraction. She is also meant to be haunted.

Several ghosts have been associated with her, including that of Sir Winston Churchill, who is supposed to appear in one of the liner's staterooms at night, smoking a cigar. While this may just be a flight of fancy, a more persistent ghost is meant to belong to John Pedder, a 17-year-old sailor who was crushed to death by an automatic watertight door during a fire-fighting exercise in 1966. Knocking is heard from the door, and

Above: The *Queen Mary* was launched in Glasgow in Scotland on September 26, 1934. Winston Churchill is said to haunt one of the liner's staterooms.

his ghost has also been seen in the passageway. Two more ghosts are supposed to inhabit the ship, a female passenger near the ship's entrance port, and a bearded engineer in the shaft alley of the engine room. One additional ghostly phenomenon is the appearance of a child's wet footprints beside the indoor swimming pool, even though there is no water in it. While there may be something behind some or even all these stories, the suspicion remains that much of the ghostly sightings are the invention of the Californian owners of the vessel. After all, their daily "Ghosts and Legends" show complete with special ghost-like effects is a major attraction on board. As with the SS *St. Paul*, ghost stories make for an interesting story, and these are easily invented to beguile a public who are willing to believe that every strange coincidence must have a ghostly reason behind it, or that ships with a long history are necessarily the haunt of the supernatural.

Above: The liner made her maiden voyage on the Southampton to Cherbourg on May 27, 1936, winning the "Blue Ribbon" for the fastest crossing of the Atlantic.
Below: The *Queen Mary* under construction at the John Brown Shipyard in Glasgow's Clydebank. No disaster marred her construction, and she was deemed a lucky ship, although this didn't stop her from becoming linked with supernatural tales.

PHANTOM SHIPS
THE FLYING DUTCHMAN

Probably the most famous of all phantom ship legends is that of the Flying Dutchman. The term "Flying Dutchman" actually refers to the captain, not his ship. There are several variations of the story, but the most widely held is the one which describes how during the 17th century a Captain Vanderdecken of the Dutch East India Company (or Van Demien, Van Straaten, and Van der Decken as other popular variants of the captain's name are written) was returning home from the Indies to Holland when he encountered a storm off the Cape of Good Hope. He swore that he would spite God's wrath, and take his ship into Table Bay, despite anything that God and the elements could throw at him. As soon as he had spoken this oath his ship struck an uncharted rock and foundered, taking everyone down with it.

Another version has the captain ignoring the counsel of both passengers and crew and—either drunk or mad—refusing to take in sail or turn away from land. Faced with a mutiny he cut down the ringleader, then threw his body over the side. At that moment the clouds parted and a shadowy figure appeared on the boat. Unperturbed the captain tried to shoot him. In retaliation the figure laid a curse on the captain, condemning him to sail the oceans for eternity "with a ghostly crew of dead men, bringing death to all who sight your spectral ship, and to never make port or know a moment's peace."

Above: As a 19-year-old midshipman in the Royal Navy, the future George V served on HMS *Bacchante* when crew reported seeing the Flying Dutchman's phantom vessel.

The phantom of the Flying Dutchman's ship is supposed to haunt the waters off the Cape of Good Hope, and the superstition that anyone who sees the wraith of his ship will one day drown in a shipwreck of their own has become a widely-held belief. There are variations to the basic tale. The ghost ship would be seen under full sail with its masts creaking under the strain and driven forward by a tempest. If Captain Vanderdecken was seen, he was meant to have been standing bareheaded at the wheel, sailing his ship through the storm while pleading for an act of mercy that never came. A crew of skeletons danced in the rigging, encouraging the ship to sail faster and faster toward its doom. It was also suggested that it had the ability to lure other ships onto the rocks, or even sour the food and water in a vessel passing through the same waters. Other legends recount how his sailing ship would come alongside another vessel and throw a bundle of letters over. If any of the letters were opened the ship would immediately founder.

One of the first properly recorded sightings of the Flying Dutchman and his phantom ship was in 1835, when a British ship was approaching the Cape of Good Hope. Witnesses recorded that they saw the phantom ship approaching them surrounded by its own storm. It came so close that the crew feared the two ships would collide, but at the last moment the phantom ship disappeared. The most widely acknowledged sighting took place on July 11, 1881, when the warship HMS *Bacchante* encountered the ship in the same waters. One of the men on board who swore they saw the Flying Dutchman was a young midshipman, who later became King George V. As he recalled it, he saw: "A strange red light as of a phantom ship all aglow, in the midst of which light the mast, spars and sails of a brig 200 yards (183 m) distant stood out in strong relief."

In March 1939 the phantom ship was seen off the coast of South Africa by dozens of people on the shore, the majority being swimmers on Glencairn Beach, near Cape Town. Independent witnesses described what they

Left: HMS *Bacchante* was a small iron-hulled screw-powered corvette launched in 1876, one of three in her class. Only a handful of the 375 men in her crew reported seeing the phantom ship off Cape Town in 1884.

had seen, and all the accounts pointed to a ship which looked like a Dutch East Indiaman of the early 17th century—accurately described by people who had probably never seen even a picture of this type of ship. The sighting was mentioned in the *British South Africa Annual* of 1939: "With uncanny volition, the ship sailed steadily on as the Glencairn beach folk stood about keenly discussing the whys and wherefores of the vessel. Just as the excitement reached its climax, however, the mystery ship vanished into thin air as strangely as it had come." Three years later she briefly re-appeared in Table Bay, seen by four witnesses in two independent private boats. During World War II, Admiral Dönitz claimed that the Flying Dutchman had been seen by one of his U-boats while on patrol off Cape Town.

The Flying Dutchman story is similar to the German legend about a Captain von Falkenberg, who was condemned to sail the waters of the North Sea for all eternity with no means to steer his ship, while forced to play dice with the devil for his soul. An even earlier version of the legend is found in a Norse saga where a Viking sea captain called Stötte stole a magic ring from the gods. He then appeared later in the Saga's narrative as a man doomed for all eternity, a living skeleton swathed by fire and perched on the mast of a phantom black-hulled longship.

The theme of the Flying Dutchman has been used in literature and music, the best known examples being Wagner's opera *Der Fliegende Holländer* and Sir Walter Scott's *The Phantom Ship*, where the villain's name is changed to Captain Marryat. At least in Wagner's libretto the captain is allowed some reprieve; every seven years he is allowed ashore to find a woman whose love can redeem his lost soul.

Right: Dutch East Indiamen foundering in a storm, from a 17th century engraving. The vessel supposedly captained by the "Flying Dutchman" was a vessel of this type.

HMS *EURYDICE* (1878)

For centuries the waters of the English Channel have been some of the busiest in the world, and sometimes the most deadly. Bounded by Britain on one side and France on the other, the Channel has proved itself to be a dangerous place for a sailing ship in the wrong conditions. Sticking out into the Channel, like a diamond-shaped stopper over the waters of the Solent, the Isle of Wight has seen its share of maritime tragedy.

Over 3,000 shipwrecks have been recorded around its shores since Admiralty records began. However, none of these maritime disasters has proved as poignantly tragic as the wreck of the *Eurydice*, and few have produced such a persistent association with ghosts. Of the 366 men and boys on board when she was wrecked, only two survived the disaster, a tragedy which sounded a death-knell for the age of sail.

HMS *Eurydice* was a wooden-hulled 26-gun frigate, built in the tradition and style of the ships which had fought at Trafalgar almost four decades before. Launched in 1843, the 921-ton ship boasted sleek lines and an impressive expanse of sail, making her one of the fastest sailing ships in the fleet. She was also virtually obsolete as soon as she was built: the future lay in steam. The same year as the *Eurydice* was launched, Isambard Kingdom Brunel's great iron-hulled steamship the SS *Great Britain* entered service, but the naval officers who had seen service with Nelson sneered at such novelties as iron ships and steam engines. It was not until after 1850 that the Royal Navy bowed to the inevitable and began to experiment with steam propulsion. Less than a decade later, in 1859, the first ironclad warship was built, and the French *La Gloire* was followed a year later

Left: The raising of HMS *Eurydice* in the late summer of 1878. Although her hull was recovered, the vessel was broken up soon afterward.

by the British response, HMS *Warrior*. From that moment on the days of wooden sailing ships were over. A reluctant Admiralty embraced the new technology, but still had to find a use for the sailing ships which still made up a large portion of the fleet. In 1876 it was decided to convert the *Eurydice* into a training ship, so that future generations of naval ratings could learn the old ways, before they learned of the new. The work formed part of a general refit, undertaken at Whites Yard at Cowes, on the north coast of the Isle of Wight. On September 7, 1876, she was re-commissioned in Portsmouth, and started her new career as a sail training ship under the command of the highly experienced Captain Marcus Hare. On November 13 the following year, she set sail for a three-month tour of the West Indies and Bermuda stations, where her crew of young sailors could literally "learn the ropes." The deployment was considered a great success, and the now

experienced crew were considered to have fully learned their new trade. She left the Windward Islands of the West Indies on March 6, 1878, and made a fast crossing of the Atlantic, taking just 16 days to reach the English Channel. At 3 pm on March 22, she was sighted by the coastguards at Bonchurch near Ventnor, on the south-eastern side of the Isle of Wight, "moving fast under plain sail, studding sails on fore and main, bonnets and skycrappers." Captain Hare obviously wanted to demonstrate the skill of his young crew by flying into Portsmouth. The wind was from the east, so the *Eurydice* was on a steady starboard tack. She passed two other smaller vessels, just 40 minutes later off Sandown Bay, as she sped off to the north-east: the schooner *Emma* (Captain Jenkins) and a local Shanklin-based fishing boat owned by a Mr. Colenut.

Suddenly a great and savage white squall swept down the Channel from the east, its edge blackened by

Right: HMS *Eurydice* was an old wooden-hulled sailing frigate which had survived the age of steam and steel-hulled warships as a training ship for young seamen. It was the loss of such a young crew that made her sinking a particular tragedy.

a blizzard of snow and ice. The fishing boat took shelter in the lee of Culver Cliff on the north end of the bay, and Captain Jenkins reefed his sails ready to ride out the blast head on. However, according to witnesses the *Eurydice* continued on under full sail. The same eyewitnesses remember her gunports were open, ready to fire a salute as the ship slipped into Portsmouth harbor just eight miles away. She was then engulfed by the squall. One of the two survivors reported that Captain Hare had ordered the sails to be taken in as soon as he saw the approaching squall, yet the tempest approached so quickly that the crew never had a chance. The frigate was whipped round to port until she lay on a reciprocal course, then she was laid over by the blast onto her starboard side. The sea poured in through her open gunports until she lay on her beam, where she rested for a minute before sinking from sight. Almost all her crew would have been trapped below decks, or else sucked under as she went down. The young sailors on the upper deck would have been completely disorientated by the blizzard and tearing winds, but at least many would have had a chance to throw themselves clear before she went down. However, the water was icy cold, and the squall was still lashing the surface of the sea. Most of those who escaped sinking with the ship likely froze to death as they struggled toward the shore.

As soon as the squall passed, the schooner *Emma* raced to the scene to pick up survivors. Only five young sailors were still alive when they got there, and of those only two survived long enough to make it to the island's hospital. Seamen Benjamin Cuddiford and Sydney Fletcher were the lucky ones. Everyone else had been lost. In the aftermath of the disaster a salvage team raised the wreck of the *Eurydice*, recovering many of the bodies, but after the inquiry was held into the tragedy, her hull was broken up. Today only her bell remains and can be found in St. Peters Church in Shanklin, hanging almost within sight of where the *Eurydice* went down. Her loss marked the passing of an era. She was the last sail training ship in the Royal Navy, and after that the art of seamanship under sail passed into history, effectively bringing the age of fighting sail to a close. The poet Gerard Manley Hopkins composed "The Wreck of the Eurydice" by way of a memorial, a work which described one of the corpses washed up onto Sandown beach. This is an extract:

> They say who saw one sea-corpse cold,
> He was all of lovely manly mould,
> Every inch a tar,
> Of the best we boast our sailors are.
> Look, foot to forelock, how all things suit!
> He is strung by duty, is strained to beauty,
> And brown-as-dawning-skinned,
> With brine and shine and whirling wind.
> O his nimble finger, his gnarled grip!
> Leagues, leagues of seamanship,
> Slumber in these forsaken,
> Bones, this sinew, and will not waken.

Clearly the disaster had a profound effect on the national psyche, at the height of a period when the Royal Navy and its sailors were the darlings and mascots of Victorian Britain. It was inevitable that in such a melodramatic age, supernatural happenings associated with the shipwreck were recorded almost as soon as the *Eurydice* was lost. For example, that afternoon Sir John MacNiell was dining with friends in Windsor, and according to the Bishop of Ripon who was present, the old soldier suddenly went pale, and reportedly exclaimed: "Good Heavens! Why don't they close the portholes and reef the sails?" When his companions asked what the matter was he replied: "I don't know, but I just had a vision of a ship coming up the Channel under full sail with her gunports open, while a great black squall attacked her." A similar experience was had by Eleanor Beckett of Portsmouth, whose brother David was a sailor on the *Eurydice*. He was expected to visit her, bringing his sister a present from the West Indies. At around 3:50 pm that Sunday afternoon she experienced a sudden sense of profound fear and panic, and seconds later she heard footsteps on her garden path. Flinging open the door, she found her pathway empty. At the same time less than eight miles away her brother had gone down with his ship.

While premonitions and accounts of visitations at the moment of death were almost to be expected, the reappearance of the *Eurydice* herself as a ghost ship was not. However, in 1880 local Shanklin fishermen reported seeing a fully-rigged sailing ship appear off Sandown Bay, moving quickly. As it drew closer to them

Above: The *Eurydice* was caught in a giant squall which ripped into her from the north-east, swinging her round on her beam and rolling her over.

the ship then disappeared. Similar sightings took place in the years which followed, although in most cases this "phantom" can be explained away by the effects of lights, mist, and wishful minds. However, in early 1934 Commander Lipscombe, the captain of the submarine HMS *Proteus* was on the conning tower of his boat as he was returning to Gosport from an exercise in the English Channel. He was close to Dunnose Point when a sailing man-of-war appeared, as if from nowhere, and almost collided with his submarine. Lipscome was a highly reputable witness, and he claims he was unaware of the *Eurydice* story until he heard it later while visiting the Isle of Wight. No logical explanation of his sighting can be found.

Does the *Eurydice* still sail the waters of the English Channel, or are such tales merely another attempt to turn an old tragedy into a compelling ghost story? As no fresh sightings have been reported for over half a century, then one suspects the latter.

20TH CENTURY PHANTOMS:

TS *KØBENHAVEN*, SS *TRICOLOR*, USS *THRESHER*

In 1914 the Danish East Asiatic Company ordered the construction of a 3,900-ton, five-masted sailing barque from a shipyard in Leith, near Edinburgh. The result was an elegant, steel-hulled vessel 368 feet (112 m) long with a 49-foot (15-m) beam. She was also fitted with a small diesel engine, powering a single propeller. As World War I broke out while she was on the stocks, the finished ship was purchased by the Royal Navy, who used her as a floating oil tank at Gibraltar. An identical replacement ship was ordered, and this time the British picked up the bill. The result was the *Københaven*, which was launched in 1921. She was an impressive sight under a full press of sail, and spacious enough for the needs of her Danish owners, carrying a crew of 50 cadets and 10 staff. She was also regarded as a good sea boat, and had excellent sailing qualities. She entered service in 1922, and for the next six years she made several long voyages, venturing as far away as Australia, the Americas, and the African coast. She was easily identifiable, as the *Københaven* was the only five-masted sailing ship afloat. However, her career came to an abrupt end after just six years.

On December 14, 1928, she set sail from Buenos Aires in Argentina and headed down the estuary of the River Plate, bound for Melbourne in Australia via

Above: The five-masted Danish ship *Københaven* was lost somewhere off the coast of South America, but her wraith was supposedly seen several months later.

Above: The *Kobenhaven* carried a crew of 50 Danish cadets when she sailed from Montevideo in December 1928. Neither they nor their ship were ever seen again, except as a ghostly apparition.

Callao in Peru. Her planned route was down through the South Atlantic and then around Cape Horn. That afternoon she passed Montevideo, on the northern Uruguayan side of the estuary, steering west-south-west toward the open sea. The *København* was never seen again. Her commander, Captain Anderson, was an expert seaman, his ship was equipped with radio, and his 60-man crew of cadets and staff was trained to deal with all eventualities.

The reason for her loss remains a mystery, but three widely-held theories emerged. One was that she was overwhelmed by a pampero, the sudden squalls which sometimes get whipped up after warm air from the pampas steppes hits colder coastal air from the Antarctic. Another theory is that she collided with an iceberg and sank with all hands, while a third suggests her ballast shifted in a storm, and she capsized.

Months after her disappearance, a five-masted sailing ship was sighted off the coast of Chile near Valdivia, on the far side of Cape Horn. A few weeks later the vessel was seen again, this time a few hundred miles to the north off the Peruvian coast south of Callao. A third sighting was reported a month later off Easter Island, hundreds of miles to the west. This might have made sense if it was the real ship, keeping to its intended course. However, the sightings began in early

Below: The Wilhelmsen fleet had a number of vessels named the *Tricolor* which came to abrupt ends. The first was built in 1904 and was wrecked in fog in 1905 off California. Their second was built in 1906, sold to Germany in 1925, and sunk by British aircraft in 1944. The company lost their third *Tricolor* in 1931, and the fourth (below), launched in 1933, eventually succumbed to a fire on its way to Oslo in 1956.

1930, over a year after the last sighting of the *Københaven*, and long after her crew had been given up for lost. As she was the only five-masted sailing ship in the world, there was no confusion over her identity. All those who saw the ship described her as the *Københaven*. After ruling out all other solutions apart from the supernatural, the only explanations for these sightings was either that all the witnesses had been lying in order to gain the limelight for a few days, or that what they saw really was the *Københaven*, only she had been abandoned by her crew and was drifting on her own. This last theory is seen as barely possible, as Captain Anderson would only have abandoned ship if she was in imminent danger of sinking; taking to the lifeboats was an extremely hazardous undertaking in rough weather. Does this mean the ship managed to round Cape Horn successfully? If she did, then why had she not radioed reports of her progress to the wireless stations on the Falkland Islands and Tierre del Fuego? Also, the chances the ship would avoid all storms, coasts, and other hazards for so long would be virtually negligible. Did the *Københaven* become a phantom ship, or were these sightings just opportunistic stories? All we know for sure is after these three sightings, the ship or its wraith never reappeared.

Another even more perplexing account of a phantom ship appeared in the June 1958 edition of *Proceedings*, the prestigious monthly magazine of the US Naval Institute. It told the story of the *Tricolor*, a 6,000-ton Norwegian merchant vessel belonging to Wilhelmsen Shipping, a small shipping management company owned by Wilhelm Wilhelmsen of Oslo. During the late 1920s she plied between Europe and the Far East, carrying manufactured goods such as furniture, industrial equipment, chemicals, and even clothing on her outbound voyages, and returning from South-East Asia with cotton, rice, and rubber. In mid-November 1930, the *Tricolor* sailed from Oslo under the command of Captain Arthur Wold. The vessel stopped in Hamburg, Dunkirk, and Rotterdam to pick up a cargo of chemicals, as well as a dozen passengers. By late December she was passing through the Suez Canal, and on January 5, 1931, she put into Colombo in Ceylon (now Sri Lanka). After taking on a small cargo of rubber she returned to sea that afternoon, only to run into the middle of a tropical storm. What followed is unclear, but somehow the ship caught fire, possibly through carelessness or else by means of a lightning strike. After sending out distress messages the majority of the passengers and crew abandoned ship. Only Captain Wold, the wireless operator, and two others stayed behind to continue transmitting for as long as possible. Their valiant efforts were proved worthwhile when the passing French liner SS *Porthos* came and rescued the survivors in the lifeboats. They were unable to save the men left behind; before they could be reached the chemicals in the hold exploded, and the ship was blown apart. There the story should have ended, but there was a postscript.

Five years later, on January 5, 1936, the British freighter SS *Khosuru* bound from Bombay to Calcutta was passing close to Ceylon through the same waters.

Sailors on board later testified to being all but run down by another ship which seemed to materialize out of a thick belt of rain. To the observers on the *Khosuru* she appeared to be deserted, with no sign of helmsman or lookouts. She passed within a hundred yards of the British freighter's bow, and as she passed, the officer of the watch, Third Officer Robinson, noted the name on her stern. It read *Tricolor*.

Unaware of the fate of the Norwegian freighter exactly five years before, the men on the bridge of the *Khosuru* railed at the un-seamanlike behavior of the Norwegians, failing to post lookouts in such poor conditions. The *Tricolor* disappeared from site again amid the rain belt. After about five minutes the weather cleared, and visibility improved well enough to see for six miles (ten kilometers) or more. The captain ordered Robinson to fix the ship's position in order to report the incident, and in so doing he had cause to look at the chart. It showed a wreck symbol, and beside it the caption: "Motor ship *Tricolor* with cargo of chemicals exploded and sank at this point at 5 pm on January 5, 1931." He looked up, and could see no sign of the *Tricolor*. Had the entire bridge crew of the *Khosuru* seen a phantom ship, or were they all lying?

Below: The nuclear-powered submarine USS *Thresher* (leading the group below) disappeared with all hands on April 10, 1963, some 500 miles off the coast of Massachusetts. Four years later a family fishing party claimed to have seen her in approximately the same location.

There is one more explanation. Wilhelmsen Shipping ordered a replacement vessel to be built, which was also called *Tricolor*. Although a little larger that the original, she was of the same general appearance. From 1936 on she covered the same route, from Oslo to South-East Asia. It is quite possible that the ship the *Khosuru* saw was in fact the second *Tricolor*, not the wraith of the first. As such, the incident is one of the most astounding coincidence rather than a ghost story. The reason the crew of the *Khosuru* failed to see the *Tricolor* after she passed was that her course coincided with that of the band of rain and she remained hidden, or that, due to light refraction caused by the passing rain, the ship was hidden from view. Whatever the reason, the crew of the *Khosuru* were unsure of exactly what almost ran them down that afternoon, five years on from the original sinking and in the same small patch of the Indian Ocean.

A more modern account of a phantom ship concerns the nuclear-powered submarine USS *Thresher*.

Below: The *Thresher* submarine which was the victim of a possible hoax sighting after its disappearance in 1963. There were some obvious contradictions in the story of the supposed witnesses to this phantom ship.

In the summer of 1967 a family from Massachusetts decided to motor out to the deep sea fishing ground near the edge of the Atlantic continental shelf. They cut engines roughly 220 miles (353 km) due east of Cape Cod in Massachusetts, and 170 miles (272 km) due south of Cape Sable in Nova Scotia. Shortly after 9 am they heard a noise and watched as a submarine broke the surface about half a nautical mile away. They made out the name "Thresher" painted on the side of the conning tower, and above it the bridge crew seemed to be scanning the horizon with binoculars. The boat seemed to be in difficulty, as she was wallowing in the swell, and had a long gash running down the side of her outer hull. As they watched the boat seemed to rise out of the water, then fall back beneath the waves. The family made enquiries and discovered a submarine called the USS *Thresher* (SSN-593) did indeed exist, except that it was lost with all hands in roughly the same patch of water (41.46°N, 65.03°W) on April 10, 1963, over four years before the family saw her re-appear. While this sounds like an incredible story, there are some serious flaws. First, the submarine never carried her name emblazoned on her conning tower, only her pennant number, "593." Also the latest theory about her loss was that for some reason the reactor shut down. Unable to use her electric motors due to her depth she tried to surface, but the air flow to her ballast tanks froze (a fault discovered in later testing), and the boat descended to her crush depth, then imploded. The accident was reported on national television and the newspapers, so even four years later there can be few Americans who were unaware of the story. While some phantom ship sightings are hard to explain, this one is almost certainly a grim hoax, and one which must have caused pain to the relatives of the 129 sailors and civilian contractors who lost their lives in the *Thresher*.

NAUTICAL MYSTERIES

THE EMPTY OCEAN

Anyone who has encountered a winter storm in the Atlantic or a hurricane in the Caribbean will be no stranger to the unpredictable power and ferocity of nature. Those who have traversed the world's oceans will also understand its scale. As a salty old treasure hunter once put it: "There's a lot of ocean out there." The largest of ships can be dwarfed by the immensity of the empty ocean, and the psychological effect this can have on sailors is ably demonstrated by the case of Donald Crowhurst and the *Teignmouth Electron*. It is also easy to see how this potentially dangerous environment can encourage the search for sinister or cataclysmic explanations for otherwise explicable mysteries involving ships that have been abandoned or gone missing.

Accounts of ships which have been abandoned on the high seas are more common than most people think. Hundreds of cases are recorded, but in most cases an explanation for the crew leaving the ship has emerged. One example of this is the case of the *Zabrina*, a Falmouth-based sailing schooner which was found hard aground on the beach near Dielette, on the western side of the Cherbourg Peninsula. When the vessel was

discovered soon after dawn on October 17, 1917, she appeared to be undamaged, but there was no sign of her crew. She had sailed from Falmouth two days before, after making at least one earlier attempt to leave port which had been thwarted by heavy seas and contrary winds. The weather front had passed, and the vessel should have made a fast passage to her destination, the small port of St. Brieuc, halfway along the north coast of Brittany. At first it was suggested she had been attacked by a German U-boat, and in these days of unrestricted U-boat warfare, this made sense. However, meteorologists later reported a sudden local resurgence of the storm, making it impossible for any U-boat to operate. The likelihood is that her four-man crew were swept overboard while trying to control their vessel, hauling in the sails on her exposed deck, or battling to avoid broaching in the oncoming waves. If that had happened, an analysis of the likely path taken by an abandoned vessel during the storm would have brought her ashore on the Normandy coast in the vicinity of where she was actually found. Other less mysterious cases were solved when the crew were either rescued, or their bodies were washed ashore. After eliminating instances where a definite or even an irrefutably logical explanation can be found, only a handful of cases remain which have defied any attempt to explain what happened.

The same holds true of ships which go missing. Since 1862 when Lloyds of London first kept detailed registers of such cases, just over 4,000 vessels have been listed as missing without trace. Many of these involved

OH! GOD PRESERVE THE MARINER,

SUNG BY
M.R PHILLIPS,
WRITTEN BY
CHARLES JEFFERY'S.

Above: Sailors are aware that in a bad storm or in dangerous waters, freak waves and unpredictable squalls can threaten to swamp or capsize a vessel with little or no warning.

wartime losses, ships which were notoriously unseaworthy, or simply ships which were overcome by catastrophic storms, typhoons or hurricanes. However, a few stand out as being particularly enigmatic, or where the definitive explanation of what happened has never been revealed. While other ships could be included in this selection of cases, the following mystery ships remain among the most perplexing or dramatic. For that reason they have the most enduring fascination as unexplained mysteries of the sea.

THE ULTIMATE NAUTICAL MYSTERY:
THE *MARY CELESTE* (1872)

Probably the best known nautical mystery is that of the sailing schooner *Mary Celeste*. In December 1862 the vessel was found drifting and abandoned some 600 miles (960 km) from the coast of Spain. She seemed in perfect condition, and nobody could find a reason why her passengers and crew should have left her. Their fate has never been adequately explained, although there have been no end of theories. It remains one of the most enigmatic stories of the sea.

The *Mary Celeste* was a wooden-hulled sailing ship, a brigantine (although she was described as a half-brig by the Board of Inquiry), with an overall length of 103 feet (31 m) and a displacement of 282 tons. She was built in the Spencer Island Yard in Nova Scotia, and began life in 1861 as a Canadian vessel called the *Amazon*. After running aground off Cape Breton seven years later she was sold at a salvage auction to a New York consortium of three businessmen, who purchased her for $3,000. They had her extensively repaired, then renamed her, registering her in New York. She therefore sailed under an American flag. She was typical of thousands of small sailing ships of her time, and apart from her grounding, nothing untoward can be found in her career before she set sail for Europe on the voyage which would end in mystery.

The owners, Messrs. Winchester, Goodwin, and Briggs appointed 37-year-old Captain Benjamin Briggs to command their vessel. He was an experienced mariner, having commanded several vessels before he assumed the captaincy of the *Mary Celeste*. In the years before the Civil War, the Massachusetts-born skipper had commanded the Boston brig *Sea Foam*, but by 1862 he had advanced to command a three-masted schooner called the *Forest King*, which was also registered in Boston. He married Sarah E. Cobb, the daughter of a Bostonian minister in the same year, and the couple sailed to Europe in the *Forest King* by way of a working honeymoon. By 1865 he had transferred command of the schooner to his brother, Arthur Briggs, and instead took up command of the bark *Arthur*, whose home port of New Bedford was closer to the Briggs family home in Marion, Massachusetts. His decision may have been influenced by the birth of his son Arthur in the same year. In 1866, the couple took their infant with them when they sailed to Marseilles in France, and Briggs may have been joined by his wife on other shorter voyages. This was a common enough practice at the time; wives and families were known to accompany the captains of small sailing ships. In 1870 when Sarah Briggs gave birth to a daughter named Sophie, Captain Briggs made plans to retire from the sea, and to go into business with his brother in New Bedford, but for some reason the scheme never materialized. It was at that juncture that Captain Briggs was approached by the

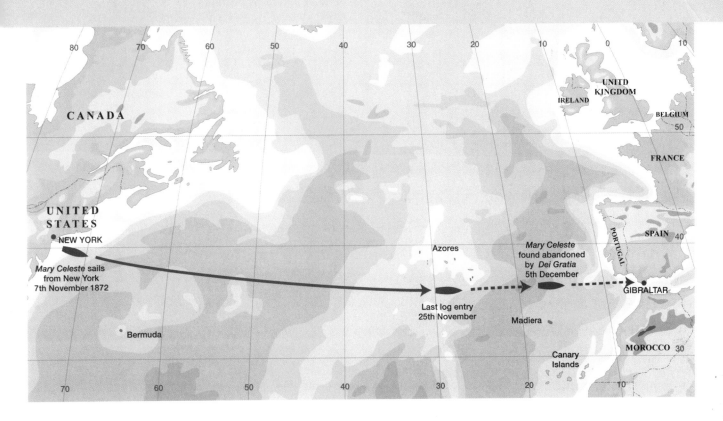

owners of the *Mary Celeste*. He purchased an interest in her, which allowed him to ship a small amount of cargo on her "of his own accord." No doubt he thought it would help provide a secure nest egg for his family. He also had the cabin of the *Mary Celeste* remodeled to better suit the need of his growing family, which he planned to take to sea with him. It was now the late summer of 1872.

From his letters it appears Briggs took no part in the refurbishment of the *Mary Celeste* but he certainly oversaw its loading with a cargo of 1,701 barrels of "American alcohol" (presumably whiskey) shipped on behalf of the firm of Meissner Ackerman & Co. to clients in Genoa, on the north Italian coast. The cargo offered no temptations to Briggs, who was devoutly religious and a firm teetotaler. By November everything was ready, and shortly before he sailed he wrote to his

mother in Marion, who was looking after young Arthur, (who was now old enough to attend school). Nothing in his letter suggested anything untoward was on his mind. From the Board of Inquiry we know that Captain Briggs invited Captain Morehouse of the brig *Dei Gratia* to dine on board shortly before he sailed.

The *Mary Celeste* sailed from New York on November 7, 1872, Captain Briggs (accompanied by his wife Sarah and daughter Sophie), an experienced First Mate Albert Richardson, and a crew of six: the Danish-born Second Mate Andrew Gilling, an American Ship's Cook Edward Head, and four German immigrant seamen: Arian Martens, Gotlieb Gondeschall, and two brothers, Volkert and "Boy" Lorenson. Neither Captain Briggs, his family or his crew were ever seen again.

The *Dei Gratia* sailed from New York a week after the *Mary Celeste*, bound for the Mediterranean with a cargo of petroleum. On the afternoon of December 5, 1872, the *Dei Gratia* had reached a point midway between the Azores and the south-western tip of Portugal, when Captain Morehouse overhauled a brigantine which he soon recognized to be the *Mary Celeste*. Incidentally, some accounts give the date of her finding as December 4, an error presumably caused by the difference between logs kept in regular time as on land, and marine time, based on noon observations of the sun. Until the late 19th century, noon marked the traditional beginning of a new day at sea. As he drew closer he realized the headsails were causing the *Mary Celeste* to head up into the wind, then veer away again, a sure sign that no experienced mariner was at her helm. When the *Dei Gratia* came close enough, Captain Morehead lowered a boat and went over to investigate. He found the vessel to be deserted.

Much has been written about meals left half eaten and still warm, and clocks set to run backward. None of this was ever mentioned at the Board of Inquiry which was subsequently held in Gibraltar. The following facts were given. The vessel was found to be in a seaworthy condition, although clearly she had rolled around in the swell for some time, causing some minor damage. The lower hull was partly filled with water, suggesting a leak. However, the foredeck hatch was missing, so in rough seas a large quantity of water could have shipped on board after the vessel was abandoned. Captain Morehouse had the impression that Briggs and his fellows had abandoned their ship in a hurry, as the crews' oilskins were left behind. He surmised they must have thought their ship was sinking. He recalled that for several days before discovering the abandoned ship, the seas had been rough, and a strong gale had been blowing, accompanied by squalls of rain.

The ship's compass was water damaged, and the chronometer and sextant were missing, along with all the ship's papers. The last entry on the log slate read November 25, just ten days before, when the *Mary Celeste* was passing the Azores. The same water damage extended to the rest of the ship. Morehouse recalled that "the Captain's bed was not fit to sleep in and had to be dried," as the skylight above the main cabin had been left open. All clothing and bedding throughout the ship was in a similar condition. Her cargo appeared intact. More importantly, all the ship's boats had gone. While Captain Morehouse was hard-pressed to recall how many boats the *Mary Celeste* usually carried, she was equipped with at least one, if not two. Deep axe cuts in the hatch cover, where the main boat would have been stored, probably indicated that the crew had used an axe to cut the boat loose rather than waste precious minutes unlashing her and launching her in a more conventional manner. Several ropes were also seen hanging over the side of the ship, possibly indicating the passengers and crew might have used them to scramble into the boats. One of these, the main halyard was trailing astern of the ship, and appeared to have been parted.

The *Dei Gratia* continued on to her destination port of Gibraltar, while Morehouse's First Mate Oliver Deveau and a small crew followed in the *Mary Celeste*, her one serviceable pump working non-stop. The Judge at the Board of Inquiry later praised Morehouse and his crew for their skill and courage in bringing the *Mary Celeste* safely into port. The Board of Inquiry was held in Gibraltar on December 18, just over four weeks after the two ships entered port. The Judge concerned himself with the incident itself, and refused to speculate on the fate of the crew. The clear explanation was that Captain Briggs had decided to abandon ship, and took to the boats. Beyond that the Judge neither knew nor cared. Their main concern was the fate of the vessel and her cargo, which did eventually reached Genoa. However, others have been more than willing to propose their own theories.

Below: This depiction of the *Mary Celeste* shows the schooner with the sail configuration she had when she was discovered, but it also shows her maintaining a steady course and speed. In fact when encountered by the *Dei Gratia* the *Mary Celeste* was drifting under jib and foremast headsails, with her bows repeatedly pointing into the wind then falling back.

Above: The *Mary Celeste* was wrecked off the coast of Haiti in 1884 and her remains have recently been located. The theory is that the owners deliberately wrecked the boat in order to dispose of the problem ship.

At the time the mystery of the *Mary Celeste* went virtually unnoticed. It was not until 1884 when the Edinburgh writer Dr. Arthur Conan Doyle wrote about her in a short story that the case reached the attention of the public. The man who would later invent the character of Sherlock Holmes did his homework, but as his story was portrayed as fiction rather than fact, he felt free to make the case seem more mysterious than it actually was. He also changed the vessel's name to the *Marie Celeste*, a nomenclature which has confused people ever since. While Conan Doyle suggested several

possible explanations, but left the reader to make up his own mind, the fate of the crew remained a mystery. Other theories followed, ranging from an attack by sea monsters, an assault by pirates to an abduction by aliens.

Of the more commonly held notions, four are the most widely cited. First, the largely German crew mutinied against the Captain, killed Briggs and his family, then took to the boats. As there was no traces of a struggle or blood on board, this is unlikely. A rusty sword was found on the ship, and some turned "red with rust" into "red with blood." Its discovery sounded no alarm bells at the time. Even more telling, Briggs was known as a good and fair captain, and his First Mate was both well-liked by his peers and highly experienced. A mutiny would also be extremely unlikely to develop on such a short transatlantic voyage. This is linked to the second theory, that everyone on board the *Mary Celeste* was killed by the crew of the *Dei Gratia* in an act of premeditated piracy, and they then concocted the story of the abandoned vessel in order to claim salvage rights on her. Not only is this extremely unlikely— Captain Morehouse went on to have a distinguished career as a captain—but also the Board of Inquiry found no evidence whatsoever that there had been any foul play.

Another popular theory concerns natural phenomena. According to weather records and the account of Captain Morehouse of the *Dei Gratia:* the seas were rough in that part of the Atlantic when the *Mary Celeste* met her fate. No leak was found in the ship's hull, so the large amount of water which had entered the vessel must have entered through her open hatches, and seeped down companionways and vents. While this was not enough to make an experienced Captain abandon his ship, it might show that she shipped more water than was normal, particularly if it took place in a matter of seconds. More spectacularly, she could have encountered a seismic tremor, underwater eruption or "sea quake," which would have accounted for the water, and might explain why her crew abandoned her because they imagined her cargo could explode. These theories are usually mentioned in conjunction with two other

"THE APPEARANCES OF THE TABLE SHOWED THAT FOUR PERSONS HAD RISEN FROM A HALF-EATEN MEAL TO LEAVE THE CABIN FOR EVER."

Above: One of the more persistent myths was that the remains of a half-finished meal lay on her cabin table. In fact this was an embellishment by Arthur Conan Doyle.

facts. First, when the alcohol was delivered in Genoa, several of the barrels were damaged, and were empty. This amounted to about 500 gallons, which was far too great a quantity for anyone to drink. Visible inebriation in any of the crew would have incurred the wrath and suspicion of the Captain, who was an advocate of temperance. Therefore if nobody drank the alcohol, it must have spilled into the scuppers of the ship. The second fact concerned her hull. John Austin, the Marine Surveyor who inspected the ship on behalf of the Board of Inquiry reported: "On approaching the vessel I found on the bow, between two and three feet above the water line on the port side, a long narrow strip at the edge of a plank under the cat-head cut away to the depth of about three eighths of an inch and about one and a quarter inches wide for a length of about six to seven feet (1.8–2.1 m). This injury had been sustained recently and could not have been effected by weather or collision and was apparently done by a sharp cutting instrument continuously applied through the whole length of the injury. I found on the starboard bow but a little further from the stern of the vessel a precisely similar injury at the edge of a plank but perhaps an eighth or tenth of an inch wider, which in my opinion had been effected simultaneously and by the same means and not otherwise. However; as the Official Surveyor for this Court of Inquiry, I must profess intense bewilderment as to the tool used to cut such marks and why they would have been cut in any vessel at these locations."

There have been some who blame sea monsters or a collision with an uncharted reef; others have suggested that the ship encountered a sea quake, and debris from the seabed could have struck the ship, causing the barrels to broach. This inexplicable damage might have been enough to make Captain Briggs lead his family and crew to the boats.

Apart from the cause, this theory is little different from the next one, which was the solution favored by both Captain Morehouse and the Board of Inquiry. Something caused the Captain to abandon ship, but rather than risk their fate on the open sea, Briggs would have preferred to rig a tow, so the boats trailed behind

the *Mary Celeste*. Whatever the cause of the abandonment was, it seemed as if Briggs intended to reboard his ship after the crisis had passed. If the towline parted, as suggested by the frayed halyard, then the boats would have been cast adrift in mid-Atlantic, probably at the height of a strong gale. They would never have stood a chance. A story circulated that five months later two rafts were discovered off the coast of Spain, with five corpses on board, one clutching an American flag. The story cannot be verified, and even if it were true, the cadavers were too fresh to have been those of the *Mary Celeste*'s crew. Of all the theories, the one about the crew temporarily abandoning ship then being cast adrift makes the most sense, and is the most pitiable. While we may never know the truth, all the evidence suggests that the crew abandoned their ship in a hurry. Exactly why they did so has never been explained, and probably never will.

As for the *Mary Celeste* herself, she was unable to tell her story. She was duly sold by her owners to pay the salvage costs, and under new ownership she resumed her career as a cargo-carrying brig based in Boston. She retained her tarnished image, and sailors being notoriously superstitious, she was never a success, as many refused to sail in her, or have their cargo transported in her hold. She changed hands several times until 1884, when she was wrecked off the coast of Haiti. Her remains have recently been located. Rumor had it that her wrecking was an attempt by her owners to rid themselves of a problem ship, and to reap the benefits of her insurance.

Above: An even more outlandish theory concerning the disappearance of the crew of the *Mary Celeste* was that the ship was attacked by pirates, who forced everyone to walk the plank.

LOST IN THE
BERMUDA TRIANGLE:
THE USS CYCLOPS (1918)

While the area known as the "Bermuda Triangle" has developed a reputation as a place where ships or planes have been known to disappear unexpectedly, few such mysteries have proved to be as inexplicable as the loss of the USS *Cyclops*. In April 1918 the US Navy collier was on a routine passage between Barbados and Philadelphia when she disappeared, leaving no clue behind to suggest what went wrong.

Interest in the Bermuda Triangle developed in the wake of the disappearance of Flight 19, a group of five Avenger torpedo bombers which disappeared somewhere off Southern Florida in December 1945. Although this was neither the first nor the last incident of its kind, it sparked sufficient interest in the history of the area that the legend of the Bermuda Triangle took root and flourished. The term "Bermuda Triangle" first appeared in print in an article in *Argosy* magazine in 1962, and it stuck. The term was derived from an earlier account of the marine losses in the area listed in *Fate* magazine (1952). Its author, George Sand, first delineated the boundaries of the area when he wrote that: "The region involved, a watery triangle bounded roughly by Florida, Bermuda, and Puerto Rico, measures less than a thousand miles on any one side." By the mid-1970s the term was in common use, and interest in the phenomenon of missing ships and planes

seemed to grow with each fresh disappearance or theory. Several new books appeared which helped ensure that public interest in the mystery remained high.

Facts are rarely allowed to get in the way of a good mystery. In 1975 Larry Kusche, a librarian at Arizona State University, investigated the claims made by these authors, and dug into the records to reveal facts that other writers had overlooked in their race to produce a sensational story. Kusche published his book, *The Bermuda Triangle Mystery – Solved*, a cogent examination of these "unsolved mysteries" which eradicated many misconceptions or inaccuracies. He discovered that rather than the area being a "Devil's Triangle" as one writer put it, the losses within the area were no greater than in any other patch of sea in North American or Caribbean waters. Many "strange" events were discovered to be perfectly explicable, and one by one he whittled the list of true mysteries down to just a handful of cases. One of these was the disappearance of the USS *Cyclops*. In effect Kusche described the Bermuda Triangle as a piece of manufactured history, where sensationalist reporting and a love of mystery helped turn a series of maritime disasters into one of the great mysteries of the sea. However, the notion of the "Devil's Triangle" refused to go away, and a fresh crop of books managed to stir the sensationalist pot in the years which

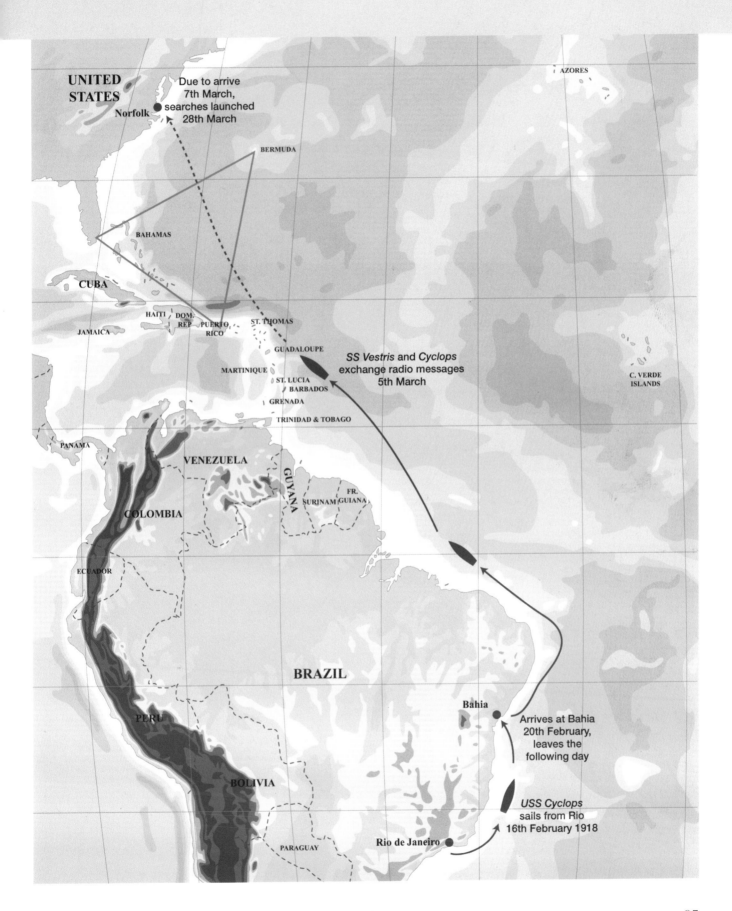

UNITED STATES

Due to arrive
7th March,
searches launched
28th March

Norfolk

BERMUDA

BAHAMAS

CUBA

HAITI DOM. REP.
JAMAICA PUERTO RICO ST. THOMAS

GUADALOUPE

MARTINIQUE

SS Vestris and *Cyclops*
exchange radio messages
5th March

ST. LUCIA
BARBADOS

GRENADA

C. VERDE
ISLANDS

TRINIDAD & TOBAGO

PANAMA

VENEZUELA

GUYANA

COLOMBIA

SURINAM FR. GUIANA

ECUADOR

BRAZIL

PERU

Bahia

Arrives at Bahia
20th February,
leaves the
following day

BOLIVIA

USS Cyclops
sails from Rio
16th February 1918

PARAGUAY

Rio de Janeiro

Above: Boats of all sizes still go missing in the area known as the "Bermuda Triangle," but most losses are due more to inexperienced mariners and untrained boat thieves than to any supernatural or mysterious forces.

followed. In order to understand the loss of the USS *Cyclops*, we need to delve into the Bermuda Triangle, to understand why the stories are so popular.

We know that since 1905 some 50 vessels of various sizes, and 20 aircraft have disappeared over the Bermuda Triangle area. While these include many cases where the loss is easily explained, such as a fishing boat or light plane caught in a hurricane, others are less readily discounted. Although writers disagree over the exact extent of the triangle, most agree that some inexplicable force within this area causes the ships and planes to vanish. Some writers (and TV producers) even

claim that the missing ships and planes are still there, only in a different dimension: the result of a magnetic phenomenon. Some even suggest that this magnetic anomaly is the work of alien creatures from another planet. A few have followed in Kusche's footsteps and sought out more rational explanations. For example, the loss of Flight 19 can be explained by compass failure resulting from the planes flying through an electrical storm. Trainee pilots flying at night, and forced to ditch in the sea, would have a poor chance of survival.

Another much-loved case is that of the SS *Marine Sulphur Queen*, a coastal tanker sailing between Texas and

Virginia, which disappeared in February 1963. Shortly before her disappearance a radio intercept placed her off Key West, south of the Florida Keys. Three days later the US Coast Guard found a lifejacket from the ship floating some 40 miles (64 km) away in the middle of the Florida Straits. No other trace of the ship was ever found. Mystery lovers made the most of this, but the more rational explanation was that the tanker was carrying a highly-flammable cargo of molten sulfur, maintained at a temperature of over 248°F (120°C). If a tank ruptured and escaping gas was ignited by a spark or cigarette, the sulfur would explode, destroying the boat and her crew in an instant. The following day the crew of a Honduran vessel in the Florida Straits reported passing through a patch of water off the western tip of Cuba where a strong, acrid odor lingered over the sea. The *Marine Sulphur Queen* wasn't the first tanker of her class to be lost in similar circumstances. Several others had tanks rupture but in these cases the crew managed to abandon ship safely. No mysterious forces were at work in any of these maritime disasters, only the unforgiving laws of chemistry.

If these and other disasters are so easily explained, why has the notion of the Bermuda Triangle persisted? One theory is that when we are faced with something mysterious, superhuman or even extra-human forces are readily found to solve the riddle, while finding a more scientific explanation takes a lot more work. Everything from UFOs to sea monsters, lost continents to gravitational anomalies have been brought into play. Meanwhile so much hokum surrounds any discussion of the Bermuda Triangle that scientists are wary of becoming embroiled in any investigation which could sully their reputation.

What scientists are willing to state is that atmospheric, magnetic, and oceanographic anomalies do exist. Meteorologists will tell you that the area is known for extremes of weather; waterspouts, tropical storms, electrical storms (known colloquially as St. Elmo's Fire), localized thunderstorms (known as meso-meteorological storms), and of course hurricanes. Some of these smaller storms can develop suddenly and with little warning, then dissipate as quickly as they came. These short-lived storms can produce violent cross-seas, huge waves, and howling squalls. Even modern satellite weather tracking can do little to predict the appearance of these storms, as they can erupt when a satellite is not overhead and able to record the phenomenon. Scientists have also proved that there are no inexplicable magnetic anomalies in the area bounded by the "triangle." What it does contain is the longitudinal line of 80° West, part of a "line" bisecting the globe where magnetic north as read on a compass and true north are exactly the same. Elsewhere there is a varying degree of difference between the two. Inexperienced navigators could easily make an error if unaware of the phenomenon.

Oceanographers can come up with an equally impressive list of natural phenomenon which effects the area. The Gulf Stream pushes north past Florida and the Bahamas at a steady four knots, shouldering its way through the colder waters of the region, and creating a series of powerful undercurrents. Most of the area

She headed south through heavy seas, and officers noted that her hull was twisting (or "working") in the swell, something they hadn't noticed before. Worley assured them the ship was perfectly seaworthy, claiming: "She'll last as long as we do."

bounded by the "triangle" consists of water which is roughly 20,670 feet (6,300 m) deep; its western side contains the North American continental shelf, which includes offshoots like the Grand Bahama Bank. Here the water is often less than 100 feet (30 m) deep, with a number of deeper channels, creating deep-water passages such as the Florida Straits and the Bahamas' Exuma Sound. Just north of Puerto Rico in the Greater Antilles, is the Milwaukee Deep or Puerto Rico Trench, which is over 30,183 feet (9,200 m) deep. Where one level of seabed meets another, sub-surface currents and thermal layers tend to collide, causing disturbances in the waters above them, which in turn can have an impact on the sea state on the surface when they come into contact with winds of varying temperatures. The result can be an area where rough seas can develop when the wind changes. What all this amounts to is that this is an area where nature's own forces are unpredictable, and where inexperienced sailors and

aviators need to be aware of their surroundings, and wary of changes in conditions. The area is a busy patch of water, with tens of thousands of ships and planes traversing it every year. The odd loss through error, inexperience, or natural phenomenon is to be expected, and need not be the subject of irrational theorizing.

While this might help explain and strip away much of the hokum surrounding the Bermuda Triangle, it fails to help explain what exactly happened to the USS *Cyclops*. Of all the mysteries of the area, this case has remained the most perplexing. Colliers played a vital role in the maintenance of an ocean-going fleet, and as the US Navy expanded during the decade before World War I, a small fleet of coal-carrying ships was commissioned to serve the needs of the fleet. The USS *Cyclops* was one of these vessels. Launched in Philadelphia in 1910, she was one of seven ships in her class, each displacing 10,000 tons, and with a strong steel hull 542 feet (162 m) in length and 65 feet (20 m) across the beam. She was designed to carry 10,000 tons of coal, and the replenishment of warships was assisted by a series of seven loading cranes on either side of her deck. Her coal stocks were sufficient to keep a U.S. battleship squadron at sea during a transatlantic voyage. Classified as being part of the Navy, she was actually run by the US Naval Auxiliary Service, and was manned by what amounted to a civilian crew. These men developed a reputation for rowdiness compared to the bluejackets of the regular fleet, but nobody questioned their ability to do their job, and in 1917 the *Cyclops* held the fleet record for fast coaling.

Above: The 590-foot long freighter *Sylvia L. Ossa* and her 37-man crew were lost at sea off Bermuda in 1976. No satisfactory explanation for her loss has emerged.

The commander of the *Cyclops* was Captain George Worley, a German-born mariner of considerable experience. Since 1890 when he took American citizenship he had served in the US Naval Overseas Transport Service, the forerunner to the wartime Naval Auxiliary Service, and had worked his way up through the ranks. In 1910 he was given command of the *Cyclops*, and took charge of her as soon as she was completed. When World War I broke out in August 1914 Worley made little effort to hide his German sympathies, even though his anti-Allied views were generally unpopular within the service. The *Cyclops* accompanied the first troop convoy from America to Britain, but after that was kept in American waters, a deployment the crew blamed on their captain's pro-German sympathies. A more likely reason was Worley's eccentricities. During his final voyage he was known to pace the bridge with a walking cane in his hand and wearing just a derby hat and his long johns! His moods were also temperamental, and his anger was legendary. He was also known as a mediocre seaman, and an indifferent navigator. In late December 1917 the *Cyclops* was ordered south to Bahia in Brazil to deliver a cargo of coal to the Allied depot, and collect a cargo of manganese ore, used in the manufacture of weapons. Despite a hernia he remained in command for the voyage, sailing from Norfolk, Virginia on January 8, 1918. She headed south through heavy seas, and officers noted that her hull was twisting (or "working") in the swell, something they hadn't noticed before. Worley assured them the ship was perfectly seaworthy, claiming: "She'll last as long as we do."

On January 13, a disagreement between Worley and his Executive Officer led to the latter's confinement in his cabin, a punishment meted out to another junior officer later that evening. The ship's surgeon would write

home from Brazil, saying he would like nothing better than to leave the ship. Clearly discipline was a problem on board. When the ship reached Bahia in late January, the *Cyclops* replenished the coal stocks of the cruiser USS *Raleigh*, then continued south to Rio de Janeiro, arriving in early February. A day out from port the collier developed engine trouble, and it soon became clear that the starboard steam system could only be repaired back in Norfolk. Until then the *Cyclops* would have to make it home as a one-engined ship.

She embarked her cargo of 10,800 tons of manganese ore, while she still retained 1,500 tons of

Below: The USS *Cyclops*, photographed during World War I. She remains the largest vessel to disappear within the area bounded by the "Bermuda Triangle," and numerous theories have circulated to explain her loss in 1918, including a fire, a freak storm, or enemy action.

coal to feed her engine, making her extremely heavily laden. Although her hull rode lower in the water than usual, lading experts decided she was a stable ship, and she was perfectly safe. She left Rio on February 16 arriving in Bahia four days later, where she took on board 72 Navy and Marine personnel, bringing her total complement to 304 men. She departed Bahia late on February 21, and set course for Barbados, which she reached on March 3. Although there was no real need, Worley decided to augment his coal stocks with an additional 600 tons, which meant that when she sailed from the island her displacement was even greater than when she had sailed from Rio. Worley put to sea again the following morning, inexplicably heading south at first before curving round toward Norfolk. This was a common event, as Worley often countermanded the orders of his navigator and set his own course. The ship had twice steamed several miles past Bahia for just that reason. During the morning of March 5, the liner SS *Vestris* passed within sight of the *Cyclops* to the north of Barbados, and the two radio operators exchanged pleasantries. The *Cyclops* then disappeared over the northern horizon, never to be seen again. She was expected to arrive in Norfolk around March 7, so when there was still no sign of her five days later, radio messages were sent, requesting her to report her position. There was no reply.

By the March 28, the Navy had become worried enough to launch a search of the waters to the north of Barbados. Meanwhile naval intelligence officers quizzed former crewmen and the families of the sailors still

Above: Lifejackets recovered from the waters of the Florida Strait in 1963, around the time of the disappearance of the SS *Marine Sulphur Queen*.

missing in an effort to see if any German involvement could be uncovered. The German-born American consul in Rio had taken passage in the *Cyclops*, a man whose German sympathies were even better known than those of Captain Worley. Rumors began to fly, and although subject to wartime censorship, the American press began to pick up the story. The Navy began quashing the wilder rumors that the *Cyclops* had been sunk by a German submarine, or even that her crew had mutinied and sailed her to Germany. They stated: "While a raider or submarine could be responsible for her loss, there have been no reports that would indicate the presence of either." They continued to search for signs of the collier for another eight weeks before officially listing her as missing on June 1, 1918. The mystery of her disappearance was never solved.

After the war, American naval investigators discovered that no German vessel had reported sinking the *Cyclops*, nor were any mines laid in her path. Several hoaxes were perpetrated, but no real leads emerged during the years which followed. What remained were theories. Some of the more inventive included an attack by a giant octopus which dragged the ship to the bottom, or that German saboteurs had planted a bomb on board her in Rio, Bahia, or Barbados. Other theories concentrated on natural disasters, one claiming a freak wave had capsized her and another that she had been struck by a giant waterspout. A far more possible explanation suggested her cargo of manganese was ignited by an internal explosion in her hold which tore the ship apart, while another version suggests a catastrophic boiler explosion which destroyed her radio, leaving her to drift helplessly until she sank.

Another explanation was aired by a former officer of the *Cyclops*, Commander Mahlon S. Tisdale. He cited the possibility that the cargo of manganese ore might have shifted, causing the ship to roll over. This would have ripped the covers from her holds, and the collier would have filled with water and sunk within minutes, leaving little trace of her presence on the surface. He stated that during his time on board he had noticed that the ship had a tendency to develop a sudden list, a fault

Above: Sand Key Lighthouse off Key West, Florida, marking the western corner of the Bermuda Triangle.

he blamed on the design of her water tanks, which allowed water to move from one side of the ship to the other. He noticed that the covers to these tanks were rarely secured, so that in heavy seas water breaking over the upper deck could pour into the fresh water tanks. Nobody ever reported encountering heavy seas around the time the *Cyclops* was lost, but we have already discussed the ability of the region of the Bermuda Triangle to generate sudden and powerful storms. A sudden heavy list caused by water slopping around in her tanks could have caused her cargo to shift, which might then have led to her turning turtle.

In 1969, an officer who had sailed on the *Cyclops* from Norfolk to Bahia described how he had heard her hull moving, and how the deck amidships seemed to be moving as if it were "conforming to the contour of the sea." He suggested the cause of her loss was structural failure, that she had broken in two in mid-ocean. He also argued that as the ship was so heavily laden, the cargo was unlikely to shift far enough to endanger the stability of the ship. However, as the cargo would have been loaded into her midships hold, the weight might have placed an undue stress on the already weakened keel, and, even in a mild swell, the pressure would have been sufficient to break her back. This explanation might have been the last word on the subject: the well-informed verdict of one of the few officers who knew the ship well enough to comment. However, the publication of his account in a naval journal with a prestigious, but limited, circulation went unnoticed. Instead, Bermuda Triangle mania was in full flight, and his verdict was submerged by a wave of less-informed and more sensational theories which described the USS *Cyclops* as an important victim of the "Devil's Triangle."

Below: The USS *Cyclops* was an ungainly vessel, her profile dominated by her coal-loading gantry forward of her bridge. An internal explosion inside her coal-filled holds is one possible explanation for the loss of the vessel somewhere between Barbados and the coast of Virginia.

AN EDWARDIAN TRAGEDY:
THE SS *WARATAH* (1909)

While ships might sink in mid-ocean, usually some scrap of evidence remains behind to explain what happened; a life raft, scraps of ship's timbers, or else the detritus of the cargo she carried. This is particularly likely if the vessel sank close to land, or on a major shipping route. What made the disappearance of the Edwardian passenger ship *Waratah* so unusual is that she simply disappeared without trace, virtually in sight of land, astride the busy shipping lane between Durban and Capetown.

The Edwardian era (1901–10) was a period of supreme technological confidence. The experimental age of steamship design had passed, and increasingly larger and more powerful vessels were entering service, powered by engines which were considered to be thoroughly reliable. The problems of stability and hull shape which had plagued the early days of steamship design had been ironed out, and the result was a basic design of merchant steamship which would remain in use for much of the century. The *Waratah* was essentially designed as an immigrant ship, carrying emigrants from Britain to Australia. She was designed to combine the cargo-carrying qualities of a freighter or troopship to transport the bulk of her human cargo, with the elegance of the Edwardian passenger ship, where the more wealthy emigrants or other passengers traveled in the luxury expected of a passenger liner of the time. The emigrant trade to America, Canada, Australia, and New Zealand was big business in the early 1900s.

The *Waratah* belonged to the Blue Anchor Line, a highly-reputable steamship company founded by Wilhelm Lund in 1869. By the time the *Waratah* entered service the company had a half-century of experience, operating between Britain, Australia, and China. A typical voyage brought emigrants out from Europe to Australia, then the ship would return to Europe via China or India, where it collected a cargo of tea. Her design was based on the *Geelong*, another successful ship in the Blue Anchor fleet, but the *Waratah* would be a little larger, and a lot more luxurious. She was built on the Clyde in 1908 by the highly reputable shipbuilding firm of Barlay, Curle, and Company, who followed the Blue Anchor Line's specifications to the letter. When completed the 9,339-ton ship was 465 feet (142 m) long, with a beam of almost 60 feet (18 m), and was powered by two modern coal-fired engines. Named after the emblem flower of New South Wales, the *Waratah* was destined to become the flagship of Lund's company. However, the name was considered fairly unlucky. In 1848 a steamer called the *Waratah* was lost off the French coast, while two more ships of the same name were lost off Australia in 1887, followed by another in

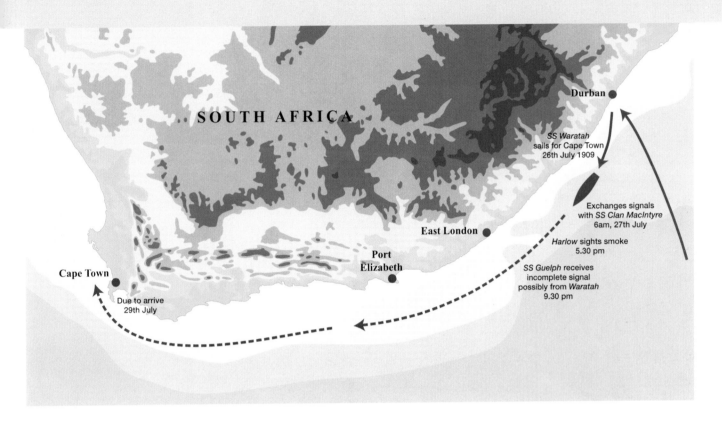

1894. Even the least superstitious shipowner would have experienced reservations in commissioning a fifth ship of the same name.

Captain Josiah Ilbery, the senior captain of the Blue Anchor Line was sent to Scotland to take charge of the vessel, and to supervise her fitting-out. A seaman with over 40 years experience, in both sail and steamships, Ilbery was approaching his retirement, and saw his new command as a fitting pinnacle of his career. The *Waratah* left the Clyde in late October 1908, then put into the Port of London to collect her first passengers. When she set sail on her maiden voyage on November 5, she carried just over 750 passengers; 67 berthed in her luxury cabins, the rest in her emigrant dormitories. She also carried a crew of 154. The ship reached Adelaide in Australia without major incident, although a small fire in a coal bunker caused Ilbery

some concern. She collected a cargo of tea, and returned to Britain a few months later, arriving back in London in late March 1909. While the return trip had been an unqualified success, Ilbery expressed concern over his new ship's performance. He noted that her stability was a problem, and that she lacked the rigidity he would have expected in heavy seas. While not as stable as the smaller *Geelong*, Ilbery said his concerns were minor ones, and there was no need for an official investigation into her seaworthiness.

The *Waratah* sailed again in late April, but this time she only carried some 215 passengers, including 22 in her cabins, and a slightly reduced crew of 119, as the lack of passengers meant there was less call for cooks and stewards on the second voyage. This time she reached Adelaide without incident, encountering smooth sailing all the way. After unloading her

> Ilbery expressed concern over his new ship's performance. He noted that her stability was a problem, and that she lacked the rigidity he would have expected in heavy seas. While not as stable as the smaller *Geelong*, Ilbery said his concerns were minor ones.

passengers she put in to several smaller ports, collecting an agricultural cargo of wheat, cowhide and lead bars before returning to Adelaide to collect passengers for her return voyage. When she left Adelaide bound for Durban in South Africa on July 7, she carried 200 passengers. She put into Durban on July 25, where she took on coal and some additional cargo, bringing her total load to just over 10,000 tons. The majority of her 200 passengers had only taken passage as far as South Africa, and a mere 92 remained on board on the evening of July 26, when she set sail for Cape Town, her last port of call before she sailed for Britain.

The two South African ports were about 600 nautical miles apart, which meant the *Waratah* was expected to arrive a little after dawn on July 29, 1909. At 6 am on July 27, she overhauled the small steamer SS *Clan MacIntyre*, which had sailed from Durban early the previous day, bound for Port Elizabeth then London. The two ships exchanged signals by lamp, the slower, smaller ship asking the larger one to identify herself. "*Waratah*, for London" came the reply. After a brief exchange, the *Clan MacIntyre*, wished the *Waratah* "Goodbye. Pleasant Passage," and the *Waratah* replied "Thanks. Same to You. Goodbye." By that time the larger faster ship had overhauled the smaller vessel, and was already pulling ahead toward the west. She remained in sight until 9:30 am, when she finally slipped over the horizon. It was the last time anyone would see the *Waratah*, her passengers and her crew; although two other vessels may have encountered her later that day, the ship they saw wasn't clearly identified though.

Later that morning the captain of the *Clan MacIntyre* signaled the keeper of local lighthouses for weather reports, but there was nothing unusual to announce. The sea was relatively calm, there was a light wind from the north-east, and there was a slight haze. The waters off the Cape of Good Hope can be notoriously fickle, however, and by mid-afternoon the *Clan MacIntyre* experienced a drop in pressure as the wind swung round to the south-west and increased in strength. By late afternoon the steamer was battling against heavy seas and a south-westerly gale, which meant her passage toward Port Elizabeth was an uncomfortable one. The same conditions were experienced by the coastal steamer *Harlow*, which was heading north-east along the coast from Cape Town to Durban. At 5:30 pm her captain sighted smoke on the south-eastern horizon, presumably from a steamer about 12 miles (19 km) off shore. At that time the *Harlow* was off the mouth of the Banshee River, south-west of Cape Hermes, the midway point between Durban and East London. In fact there was so much smoke on the horizon that he commented to the mate that he thought she might be on fire. However, as darkness fell there was no sign of a glow, only the masthead lights and stern lamp of the mystery ship,

heading toward the south-west on a reciprocal course through the heavy seas. Given their position, the lights could well have been those of the *Waratah*. They appeared to be getting closer to the *Harlow*, but around 9 pm the lights suddenly disappeared. This event coincided with two flashes, the first more powerful than the second. At first Captain Bruce of the *Harlow* thought they were explosions, but then decided they must have

Below: The *Waratah*, bearing the distinctive emblem of the Blue Anchor Line on her funnel. When she entered service in the fall of 1908 she was regarded as a well-founded ship, ideally suited for the long voyage between Britain and Australia.

been from brush fires on the shore. At around 9:30 pm the watch officer on board the Union Castle liner SS *Guelph* spotted a large passenger steamer some five miles (eight kilometers) away, and the two ships exchanged signals using their lamps. The officer on the *Guelph* had problems making out the identification signal from the other ship, and only caught the last three letters of the message; "tah." It was only with hindsight that he thought she might have been the *Waratah*.

The gale blew itself out shortly before midnight and the wind veered back to the north-east. However, the following morning the wind shifted again, and this time the south-westerly gale returned in what was described as hurricane force, one of the worst storms to lash the Cape of Good Hope for over a decade. One captain described it as the worst storm he had experienced in 13 years of sailing. Somehow all the ships in the area survived the experience, and managed to reach the safety of port over the next day or two. There was one exception. The *Waratah* was due to put into Cape Town on the morning of July 29, but by that evening she had still not arrived. Then other ships from Durban began to arrive in Cape Town, vessels which had left port after the *Waratah*, and which had traveled the same route as she had. None of these ships reported seeing the *Waratah*, and none had spotted any wreckage. It was almost as if the ship had been swallowed up. Over the next few days two tugs were sent out to search for the *Waratah*, followed a few days later by two British cruisers. No definite sign of the missing vessel was ever found, partly due to 40-foot (12-meter) waves and strong gales (conditions the press were now describing as "Waratah Weather"). However, on August 11 crewmen on the steamer SS *Tottenham* reported seeing bodies floating in the sea off the mouth of the Banshee River. The steamer's captain conducted a search of the area, but declared the "bodies" were actually pieces of whale blubber, a commonly-encountered form of waste in waters frequented by whaling ships. One of the tugs combed the area the following day, and found floating pieces of blubber, but no bodies. According to the press bodies were also spotted by the captain of another steamer, the SS *Insizwa*, bound for Cape Town. The captain elected not to stop and investigate, for fear of alarming his passengers. Captain Moore later denied the sighting, but this recantation might well have been due to the likelihood that he would have been required to remain in Cape Town pending an official inquiry into the disaster. The real truth may never be known.

While church congregations in Australia and South Africa prayed for a miracle, the press took up the story, poking around for leads which might help explain the disappearance. One newspaper ran the melodramatic story of Claude Sawyer, a British businessman who was scheduled to sail in the *Waratah* from Adelaide to London. Instead he disembarked in Durban, and refused to return on board. Sawyer claimed that during the 18-day voyage to South Africa he had been plagued by a recurring nightmare. In his dream he pictured himself standing by the steamer's rail, when the equestrian figure of a medieval knight rose from the sea beside him. The apparition was holding a sword and a blood-soaked rag, and seemed to be mouthing the words "The *Waratah*! The *Waratah*!" That was enough for Sawyer, and nothing could induce him to remain on board when the steamer reached port. He also claimed that when he mentioned his dream, Captain Ilbery sent one of his officers to tell Sawyer to keep his scaremongering dreams to himself. Once he disembarked, Sawyer sent a telegram to his wife in Britain which said nothing of the ghostly image, only that he had considered the vessel to be top-heavy, and had decided to take passage on another ship. He also reported this and a subsequent dream to the local agent of the shipping company when he booked passage on a later ship.

Below: The first class stateroom and main companionway of the *Waratah* shows the opulence that Edwardian travelers expected in their passenger ships. The quarters reserved for poorer immigrants seemed a world away from such opulent surroundings.

By mid-August hope had given way to despair, while the newsmen continued to develop ever-more outlandish theories. The ship had been taken under tow by another ship. The *Waratah* had filled her decks with coal, making her unstable. The steamer had been attacked by pirates, then scuttled.

Sawyer was a level-headed and well-respected man, but his tale proved a gem for newspaper readers steeped in Edwardian melodrama. Inevitably, they linked the knight to the story of the Flying Dutchman, whose ghostly ship was meant to inhabit the same waters. A few other first-class passengers had also mentioned that the *Waratah* rolled in an alarming way during her voyage, but the rest of the poorer passengers who had disembarked at Durban claimed they hadn't noticed anything unusual, probably because they were berthed too low down in the ship to feel any great change in her movement. Sawyer's telegram is important, as the businessman was originally trained as an engineer, and would have understood the physical laws governing maritime stability.

By mid-August hope had given way to despair, while the newsmen continued to develop ever-more

outlandish theories. The ship had been taken under tow by another ship. The *Waratah* had filled her decks with coal, making her unstable. The steamer had been attacked by pirates, then scuttled. She sank, and the survivors were living on a deserted island. She was drifting somewhere in the Indian Ocean. Clairvoyants added their own accounts of visions, one South-African spiritualist claiming she had struck an uncharted rock and sank within seconds. Although most of these theories could be discounted, the Australian government continued to fund the search for her, and hoped that against all the odds she was still afloat. Finally on December 15, the British Admiralty bowed to the inevitable and officially declared her to be "missing." A year and a day later the British Board of Trade opened an Inquiry into her loss in London. All of the theories were considered, and almost all were discounted. The court discounted the sighting of bodies in the water, and then considered the evidence from the captains of the *Harlow* and *Guelph*, but felt unable to determine any clear account of the progress of the *Waratah* after she was last seen by the *Clan MacIntyre*. Unable to produce a definitive account of what happened during those hours off the South African coast, the members of the board were forced to discount all evidence they found was contradictory or misleading.

What remained was the nagging concern over the vessel's stability. The jury considered reports from former passengers and crew, her builders, from her owners, and even from the dockside workers in Durban who had watched her sail. No concrete proof of her

Above: An artist's impression of the final moments of the *Waratah*, based on the theory that she encountered freak sea conditions off the South African coast, ploughing into a huge trough in the sea before being hit and capsized by a large wave.

instability emerged, a fact which would have proved some consolation to the owners of the Blue Anchor Line. Engineering experts reported that she was not top-heavy, and that reports that she had an excessive roll in heavy seas was not a likely contributory factor to her loss. Indeed, one naval architect stated that unless the seas had entered her holds, no tempestuous seas could have capsized her. Then Professor William Bragg took the stand. Not only was he one of Britain's leading

physicists, he would go on to win the Nobel Prize for services to physics. He had also been a passenger on the *Waratah* during her first voyage. Professor Bragg declared that he had been alarmed by the ship's behavior during the voyage from Australia to Britain, having noticed a tendency for the ship to list to starboard for several days at a time. He concluded: "My impression was that the metacenter was just slightly below the ship's center of gravity when she was upright,

> One of the final witnesses was Claude Sawyer. He declared that he had noticed a pronounced list when the ship left Melbourne, and she had a tendency to roll slowly, then snap back again. One morning he noticed his bathwater was lying at a slope of around 45 degrees!

then as she heeled over to either side she came to a position of equilibrium, where she hung for a considerable time." In other words, she heeled over easily, then stayed there, lacking the balance required to roll back again. He added he thought it a matter of luck that she had not foundered during the voyage. The shipowners brought in witnesses from the same voyage which contradicted Professor Bragg's testimony, although several other former passengers and crew supported his observations. No firm conclusions were reached, but the members of the inquiry felt that the shipowners were holding something back. Of all the evidence submitted to the court by the Blue Anchor Line, no report from Captain Ilbery appeared to have mentioned stability problems. The court declared that the silence of the late captain ran "contrary to the whole practice of the sea." As Ilbery was an

experienced mariner, the only sensible explanation was that the shipowners were covering their tracks.

One of the final witnesses was Claude Sawyer. He declared that he had noticed a pronounced list when the ship left Melbourne, and she had a tendency to roll slowly, then snap back again. One morning he noticed his bathwater was lying at a slope of around 45 degrees! However, as an engineer, what concerned him most was the tendency of the steamer to pitch into the waves, and her reluctance to rise with the swell. Rather she crashed through oncoming waves, bringing a cascade of water surging over her decks. When the rough seas abated the motion of the ship improved, and it was not until he was three days out from Durban that he began having his nightmares. A combination of his concern over the motion of the ship and the ghostly vision were enough to make him change his plans and remain in Durban when the *Waratah* sailed. He claimed the dream was repeated during the night of the July 28–29, but this time he also had a premonition of disaster. Sawyer stated that in his dream he saw the *Waratah* struggling through very heavy seas. Then a wave broke over her forecastle, pressing the streamer down by the bow, at which point she rolled over on her starboard side and went under. While the dreams can be rationalized as the subconscious fears of an experienced engineer, Sawyer was such an upstanding witness that his account disturbed those who heard his statement, and delighted the newspaper reporters covering the inquiry.

The Board of Inquiry delivered its findings on February 22, 1911. It stated that the *Waratah* had last been seen by the crew of the *Clan MacIntyre*, heading south-west. She would have encountered the storm that sprang up, and the larger one which followed it the following day. Given the nature of the vessel and the experience of her crew, it was probable that the ship was lost only through encountering a storm of extraordinary force, which had caused her to capsize. Although unable to give a reason for the ship capsizing, the court declared that they had concerns as to the stability of the *Waratah*, and recommended that a further general investigation into merchant ship stability be conducted. The verdict meant that the Blue Anchor

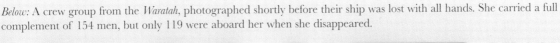

Below: A crew group from the *Waratah*, photographed shortly before their ship was lost with all hands. She carried a full complement of 154 men, but only 119 were aboard her when she disappeared.

Above: Another view of the forward stateroom of the *Waratah* and her main companionway. Given her propensity for listing, passengers would have found it difficult to relax in these comfortable surroundings.

Line was held partly responsible, and as the safety of her ships had been brought into question, passengers booked their passages with other companies. Within a year the company had been folded, and their remaining ships were sold to the Peninsular and Orient (P&O) Company.

As for the *Waratah*, her fate has never been satisfactorily explained. Most sunken vessels release debris as they break up, but no such wreckage was ever found in the years which followed the disaster. Other theories emerged, and hoaxers continued to try to sell their story, but no new evidence ever appeared. In 1936, the SS *Rabaul* steaming in the same area was caught by an unexpected gale which soon escalated into a full-blown hurricane. A gigantic wave almost swamped the ship, but it emerged unscathed. Oceanographers have subsequently confirmed that local storms of hurricane-like intensity can be produced in these waters. Another natural phenomenon encountered in the same region is the "ocean hole," a vortex created by the clash between two underwater currents. In 1964 the captain of the SS *Edinburgh Castle* encountered a large "mid-ocean cavity," which caused his ship to list heavily until it passed the hole. However, this was not considered a serious threat to the stability of his ship. Nine years later Professor Mallory of the University of Cape Town published an oceanographic paper which described this phenomenon, as well as the existence of freak 60-foot (20-meter) waves in the same patch of sea where the *Waratah* disappeared. He stated that the combination of the sharp drop of the continental shelf off the coast, the power of the Agulhas Current, and a severe south-westerly gale could produce swells which converge into waves big enough to engulf large ships. The freak wave phenomenon will probably

remain the most credible theory explaining the disappearance of the *Waratah*. If she was hit by a wave of this magnitude, her deck hatches could have been smashed in, moving her center of gravity. Given her stability record, if she was then rolled over, or encountered a cavity in the ocean, she might well have capsized and sunk within seconds. Any debris would have been swept away by the fast-moving Agulhas current, leaving no evidence of the disaster for the searchers to find.

If this indeed was the fate of the *Waratah*, the sequence of events would have been unnervingly similar to those described in Claude Sawyer's dream.

Below: The *Waratah*, photographed off Adelaide, 1909. Although her design followed that of her well-respected predecessor, she was rumored to be a poor sea boat, prone to listing in all but the calmest seas.

LOST IN THE ICE:
EREBUS AND *TERROR* (1847)

We know the first Norse explorers probed the waters west of Greenland, and that they veered south to discover America. They brought back tales of an ice-bound sea, leading away to the west. For centuries after Christopher Columbus rediscovered America in 1492, explorers were fascinated by rumors of this northern icy seaway, which was dubbed the "north-west passage." Martin Frobisher was the first to search for a way through the ice, and the task was later taken up by Henry Hudson, who died in the attempt to find the legendary waterway. By the mid-19th century the north-west passage remained one of the last great challenges of maritime exploration, and the quest attracted some of the leading arctic explorers of the Victorian age. The most distinguished of these men was Sir John Franklin, who led a new expedition into the area in 1845. He and his ships would never return, prompting one of the great mysteries of Arctic exploration. The fate of his missing ships *Erebus* and *Terror* have remained a mystery ever since.

When the Napoleonic Wars ended in 1815, Britain found itself the undisputed master of the seas. Consequently, the Royal Navy felt it had a duty to further scientific knowledge, and to map uncharted seas. Part of this drive included sending a series of expeditions in the Arctic and Antarctic, and the naval explorers succeeded in greatly furthering scientific knowledge. One of these explorers was Lieutenant John Franklin. Born in Lincolnshire in 1786, he joined the Navy as a midshipman attached to HMS *Polyphemus* in 1800. The French Revolutionary War was at its height, and Franklin soon saw action at the Battle of Copenhagen (1801). Shortly afterward he was sent to the discovery ship HMS *Investigator*, a vessel commanded by his cousin. During the voyage to Australia which followed, Franklin showed his aptitude for exploration and survey work. However, he was soon returned to larger ships, and served on board HMS *Bellerophon* during the Battle of Trafalgar (1805). By the time the war ended he was still a Lieutenant, but he had become a highly respected seaman. In 1818 he was given command of the discovery ship HMS *Trent* and ordered north to map the uncharted northern coast of Canada, part of the new drive to find the north-west passage. Although he never found a sea route to the Pacific Ocean, he did chart areas which would allow others to probe deeper into the waters north of Canada. Franklin had become something of a Victorian hero.

Franklin was promoted to Captain and then in 1829 he received a knighthood when he returned from a second north-west passage expedition which charted another 400 miles (640 km) off coast to the north of Canada. A series of naval and diplomatic appointments followed, but in 1845, Sir John Franklin was called upon

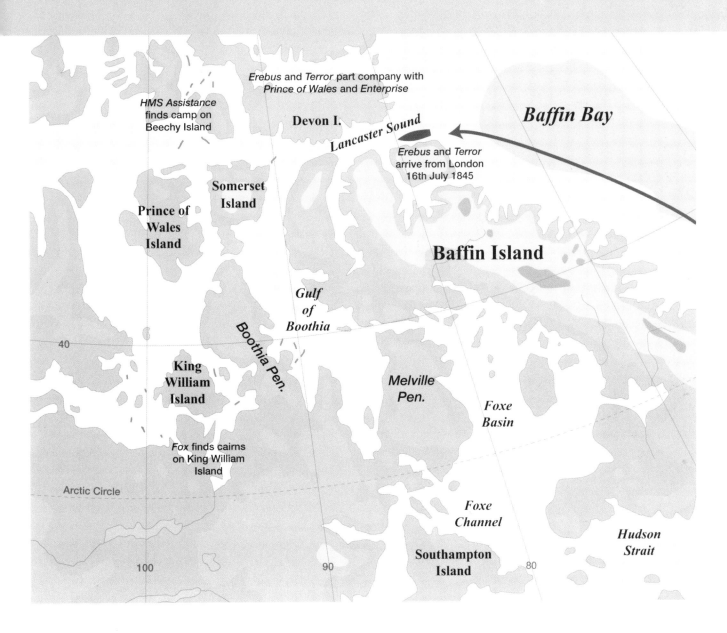

Erebus and Terror part company with
Prince of Wales and Enterprise

HMS Assistance
finds camp on
Beechy Island

Devon I.

Lancaster Sound

Baffin Bay

Erebus and Terror
arrive from London
16th July 1845

Somerset
Island

Prince of
Wales
Island

Baffin Island

Gulf
of
Boothia

Boothia Pen.

40

King
William
Island

Melville
Pen.

*Foxe
Basin*

Fox finds cairns
on King William
Island

Arctic Circle

*Foxe
Channel*

*Hudson
Strait*

Southampton
Island

100   90   80

to lead a third expedition in an attempt to locate the north-west passage. He already had the ships he needed. When James Clark's Antarctic expedition returned to Britain, his two survey ships HMS *Erebus* and HMS *Terror* were earmarked for use by Franklin. They were fitted out with steam engines and propellers, the latest in a line of major renovations for the two ships. Both were bomb vessels, designed to house large caliber mortars which could be fired from a stationary vessel against a shore target. Both displaced around 340 tons, and both were similar in design, having both been built by Sir Henry Peake. *Terror* entered service in 1815, while *Erebus* followed 13 years later in 1826. Both vessels had been converted into discovery ships by removing their ordnance and replacing their interior spaces with additional storerooms and living quarters. The theory was that bomb vessels were exceptionally well built, as they had to absorb the recoil of their large caliber

Above: Sir John Franklin (1786–1847). For years after his disappearance his wife Lady Jane Franklin never gave up hope that her husband would be found alive.

weaponry. This made them equally suited for service in icy waters, as the hulls could withstand the pressure from pack ice better than most conventionally constructed ships. The addition of steam engines simply made them more adept at forging their way through ice floes. In common with most wooden-hulled ships of the Navy, they were painted black, with a yellow horizontal strip running along their hull, marking where the line of gunports would be if they had been conventionally armed. Franklin oversaw the preparations, selected his crews, and ensured the expedition had enough provisions to last his 133 men for three years.

The expedition sailed from the Thames on May 19, 1845, and they made a swift passage to Baffin Bay off the north-eastern coast of Canada, dropping anchor there on July 26. The crews of two whaling ships, the *Prince of Wales* and the *Enterprise* witnessed the arrival of Franklin's ships as they lay off Lancaster Sound, waiting for the ice to the north of Baffin Bay to break up. The whalers and the discovery ships sailed in company for almost a week before they parted off the northernmost point of Baffin Island. When last seen the *Erebus* and *Terror* were moored to a floating iceberg, on which Franklin had set up a temporary observatory. The Scottish whalers were the last Europeans to see the two naval ships and their crews. After that they would be swallowed up by the ice of the Arctic. Back in Britain, the Admiralty fully expected Franklin to winter somewhere in the region, but by mid-1848 it had become clear that some serious misfortune had befallen the expedition. Their supplies would have been exhausted, and Franklin would have headed south to replenish his ships in some Canadian port. The British Government posted a reward of £20,000 to anyone who could locate the missing expedition, and Lady Franklin provided an additional £5,000. This was a colossal sum, and therefore no fewer that 15 relief expeditions were organized, the majority of which had no real chance of success. Few thought that the crew were lost, only that they had somehow become trapped, a fate which had befallen other Arctic explorers who lived to tell the tale. However, by the following year it became clear than none of these expeditions had found any clue to indicate where Franklin's ships were. Other expeditions followed, but it was not until mid-1850 that

Above: HMS Erebus In The Ice, a painting by François Etienne Musin from 1846. The work depicts the vessel as she might have looked during her first winter in the Arctic.

the British Naval Franklin Search Expedition led by Commodore Horatio Austin finally stumbled across Franklin's trail. On August 23 Captain Erasmus Ommanney of HMS *Assistance* found traces of a camp established by Franklin on Cape Riley, on Beechy Island, lying off the northern tip of Somerset Island. Near the detritus of the long abandoned camp they found the graves of three sailors from the *Erebus* and *Terror* who

had died during the spring of 1846. Ironically, another naval officer from the expedition, Captain McClure of HMS *Investigator* managed to climb a 656-foot (200-m) ridge near the camp; looking away to the north-west, he saw a wide channel stretched away to the west. He had found the north-west passage almost by accident.

The following spring the expedition launched a total of 28 search parties across all the islands they encountered, but no new evidence was discovered. As the news reached Britain, the newspapers published their own theories and quoted the ravings of the cranks who were attracted by the mystery. An Irish seaman claimed seeing two ships entombed in a giant iceberg in the North Atlantic, a story which tied in with a similar sighting a few months later by the crew of a German ship which reported seeing two half-submerged and waterlogged ships in roughly the same area. Like all nautical mysteries, stories fed off each other, and were made plausible by a thin veneer of information gleaned from the press.

A second official naval expedition sailed from Britain in 1852, but this time the ships ran into difficulty, becoming trapped by pack ice. Captain Belcher abandoned four of his five ships, an act which demonstrated both his lack of Arctic experience, and the danger of operating in such a hostile environment. No further official expeditions were undertaken, although several unsanctioned ones continued the search, including ones paid for by Lady Franklin, who spent all her savings trying to find what fate had befallen her husband. Finally on January 20, 1854, the British Government announced in the *London Gazette* that unless it heard any news to the contrary by the end of March, Franklin and his men would be considered to have died. It would not be until the end of the year that anyone learned any more about the fate of the missing expedition.

The Orkney-born Arctic explorer John Rae was the Chief Factor of the Hudson's Bay Company, but he also conducted his own surveying expeditions along the northern Canadian coast. While he was surveying the western side of the Boothia Peninsula, he learned from local Inuit that members of a European expedition had starved to death. It was the first real clue. Over the coming year more clues would be found, including the discovery of a backgammon set given to Franklin by his wife. By the time the news reached Britain, the country was at war with Russia, and all naval resources were needed to support the campaign in the Crimea. However, the redoubtable Lady Franklin was determined to launch one last expedition, and through public subscription she raised the funds required.

The experienced Arctic explorer Leopold McClintock led the expedition, and he chartered the 177-ton yacht *Fox* and crewed her with 25 experienced volunteers. The *Fox* sailed from Aberdeen in July 1857, and by mid-August it had reached Melville Bay, where it was caught in a fast-moving pack of ice. McClintock managed to disentangle his ship from the floe the following March, and the expedition continued. By August 1858 McClintock reached Beechy Island, the site of Franklin's winter camp. McClintock wintered in the same spot. Then, on March 1, the sailors encountered an Inuit hunting party. One of the men was wearing a brass naval button on his coat, and McClintock quizzed the Eskimos. They produced several other items, including buttons, knives, spoons, and even a medal belonging to the assistant surgeon of the *Terror*. Most had been acquired through barter with other Inuit, who had spoken of a big ship crushed by ice off King

Above: HMS *Erebus* and HMS *Terror*, accompanied by other vessels, setting out on their long voyage to the Arctic in May 1845. The two ships began their lives as bombing vessels, with specially strengthened hulls designed to absorb the shock when their ordnance was fired. The same qualities made them ideal for operating amid the ice floes of the North-West Passage.

William Island. This was close to where Rae had encountered his Inuit hunters almost five years previously. McClintock felt he was close to solving the mystery. He headed south toward King William Island, and then McClintock split his men into two teams, with the intention of meeting 600 miles (960 km) away, on the far side of the island. It was the team led by Lieutenant Dobson who found the first hard evidence.

On May 3, 1859, he came across a cairn close to Victory Point the north-west side of the island. Beneath it lay the well-preserved remains of tents, clothes, and a sextant. Two days later he found another cairn, but this time he also found a message. Written on May 24, 1847, it stated that the two ships had wintered in the ice at Beechy Island. It also reported that all was well. Clearly whatever had happened to the expedition, it occurred after that. Hobson then noticed a smaller note written in the margin. This one was dated April 25, 1848. It said: "HM Ships Terror and Erebus were deserted on 22 April, five leagues NNW of this, having been beset since 12 September 1846. The officers and crews, consisting of 105 souls under the command of Captain F.R.M. Crozier, landed here in Lat 69 deg 37 mins 42 secs N, long 98-41 W. Sir John Franklin died on 11 June 1847, and the total loss by deaths in the expedition to this date, nine officers and 15 men." It was signed by Captain Crozier. A note beneath his signature read "And start tomorrow, 26th, for Black's Fish River."

Hobson sent a message to McClintock, who joined him at once. The expedition moved south, and Inuit hunters they encountered told them that the survivors of Franklin's expedition had indeed marched south toward Black Fish's River, with men dying from starvation along the way. Three weeks after finding the second cairn, the McClintock expedition came upon the skeleton of a sailor, still wearing the uniform of a steward. He was identified as Petty Officer Peglar from the *Terror*. Having reached the southern end of the island the expedition moved north, where they came across a damaged boat. Inside it were two bodies, surrounded by a wealth of personal objects. McClintock guessed that the boat had been returning to the ships after the march south, but it had to be abandoned, along with two men who were too weak to continue. After burying the dead and collecting some of their finds, they returned to the *Fox*.

The world learned of these harrowing discoveries soon after the *Fox* entered Portsmouth in late September.

At last Lady Franklin knew her husband was dead, and had been for the past 12 years. While McClintock's expedition had provided most of the answers Lady Franklin and the public wanted, other questions were raised. Why were the ships abandoned, and where? Did any of the sailors manage to survive? Could they be living among the Eskimos, cut off from the rest of the world? The speculation continued, and is still continuing today.

The fate of the men still remains a mystery, although recent scientific evidence may provide a clue. Bone samples taken from the bodies of the men discovered by McClintock were recently analyzed, and it was discovered that all the samples had exceptionally high levels of lead in them, over ten times the level found in samples taken from the local Inuit. Most of the food supplied for Franklin's expedition came in the form of tin cans, a relatively new invention patented by a man named Goldner. An analysis of the tins recovered from Franklin's expedition have shown that they were sealed using a poor-quality lead solder. This then leaked out into the food and contaminated it. The men would never have guessed they were suffering from a combination of lead poisoning and gastroenteritis, and over time the combination would have proved fatal. While this helps explain why the men died, it doesn't reveal where they expired. Equally important, the location of Franklin's body and his two ships remain unknown. Neither the *Erebus* nor the *Terror* have ever been located, and the icy waters off King William Island continue to hold their secrets.

ALONE IN THE ATLANTIC:
THE *TEIGNMOUTH ELECTRON* (1969)

The story of Donald Crowhurst and the *Teignmouth Electron* is less a tale of nautical mystery, but rather one which demonstrates the powerful psychological effect the ocean can have on the mind. The only mystery surrounding the case concerns whether the sole victim committed suicide, or simply fell overboard.

The story began in 1968, when the *Sunday Times* newspaper sponsored a single-handed round-the-world yacht race, the Golden Globe. This was an elite sport, and the handful of men who were willing, and able, to compete needed considerable resources to supply a suitable boat, equip it, and organize a support team back home. Equally important, they also needed the frame of mind required to endure months of solitude on the high seas. Single-handed voyages of this kind had been undertaken before; the first being the American yachtsman Joshua Slocum, who claimed he encountered the ghost of a long-dead Spanish mariner in mid-ocean. The most recent was Sir Francis Chichester, who circumnavigated the globe and had returned safely back to Britain in 1967.

What was different about the *Sunday Times* competition was that it would pit some of the most experienced yachtsmen in the world against each other as well as against the elements. Five British sailors: Bill King, Chay Blyth, Robin Knox-Johnston, John Ridgway, and Nigel Tetley all agreed to take part, as did Alex Carozzo of Italy and Bernard Moitessier and Loick

Above: Crowhurst prepared the boat for departure from Devon in 1968. After he sailed, it was eight months before he was seen again by the crew of a Norwegian freighter.

Fougeron of France. The rules were simple. Competitors could choose their own time and place of departure, then had to return to the same harbor after their circumnavigation. Departure times were verified by a national newspaper, and prizes were to be awarded for the first boat home, and for the fastest round-the-world passage. A committee of experts, headed by Sir Francis Chichester, would verify the passage times, and adjudicate the race.

At the last moment another British contender elected to enter, a largely unknown entrant called Donald Crowhurst. The 36-year-old yachtsman had been born in colonial India, but brought up in Britain. After a less than distinguished career in both the Royal Air Force and the Army, Crowhurst discovered his true vocation as a research scientist at the University of Reading. The job was poorly paid, so when he married in 1957 he took up a new job as a technical salesman for an electronics firm. The job didn't last, and he eventually wound up in Bridgewater in Somerset, working for an electrical engineering firm. By this time he had a family with four children to support, and he was keen to make a success of his own business. He was already a keen amateur yachtsman, and owned a 20-foot (six-meter) sloop which he sailed in the Solent. Electronic navigational aids were in use by most yachtsmen at this time, and Crowhurst used his electronic skills to develop an improved version which he christened the "Navicator." He set up a small business to manufacture the product, and by 1964 Electron Utilisation seemed destined for success, employing six full-time staff in addition to its manager. However, gifted engineer though he was, he lacked the financial skills needed to make the company prosper. The firm was virtually bankrupt when Crowhurst met local businessman Stanley Best, who agreed to help finance the firm. The business survived, but it was still

struggling, and in early 1968 Best threatened to pull out of the partnership. Instead, Crowhurst talked him into a new scheme, which he claimed would help turn the firm around. Using Best's money, Crowhurst planned to build a trimaran to his own design, and enter it in the Golden Globe Race. By equipping it with the Navicator, and other electronic gadgets designed by Crowhurst, he expected the publicity generated would be sufficient to give the company an enormous boost.

The hull of the trimaran was built in Brightlingsea on the Essex coast, and the vessel completed at Brundall in Norfolk. The vessel was due to be completed in early September, and Crowhurst set his departure date as October 1, four weeks before the deadline which marked the last possible departure time for race entrants. The building process took longer that expected; it was not until September 23, that the trimaran was launched. He named the vessel the *Teignmouth Electron*, named after the port he had chosen as his departure point. Most of the race yachts had already sailed, and not only would Crowhurst be the last to leave, he would also be struggling to make the deadline.

The maiden voyage to Teignmouth was fraught with problems, and took over two weeks not the expected two days, largely because the trimaran proved exceptionally difficult to steer to windward. He finally set sail from Teignmouth with just nine hours to spare, limping out of the harbor because of a problem with his sails, and set a course for Cape Finisterre. He would never see Devon again.

His muddled, late departure seemed to indicate that Crowhurst was ill-prepared for the voyage ahead. Experts doubted his ability to last the course, and even questioned whether he should have taken part in the race at all. He was well behind the rest of the pack: Chay Blyth and John Ridgway had both dropped out, Robin Knox-Johnston had rounded the Cape of Good Hope, while the remaining three entrants were close behind, sailing down the African coast. The *Teignmouth Electron* had no real trial before she sailed, and from the log we know that Crowhurst was encountering problems with his boat and his equipment. At one stage he even wrote: "This bloody boat is just falling to pieces." He sent his first radio message while he was en route for

Madeira, and not long after that it appeared as if his luck had improved. After catching the trade winds his passage became swifter, and in a radio message sent on December 10, he recorded a daily run of 243 miles, which was a world record. The press were delighted, but Sir Francis Chichester remained unconvinced, describing Crowhurst as "a bit of a joker." By the New Year Italian Alex Carozzo had dropped out after developing a stomach ulcer, and Briton Bill King was knocked out of the race when his boat capsized off Cape Town, and had to be towed into port. Frenchman Loick Fougeron's boat also capsized and was badly damaged, so he too pulled out of the race. While Robin Knox-Johnston was still in the lead somewhere off

Below: On July 10, 1969, the RMS *Picardy* found the *Teignmouth Electron* drifting in mid-Atlantic. She was taken alongside the freighter for a closer inspection.

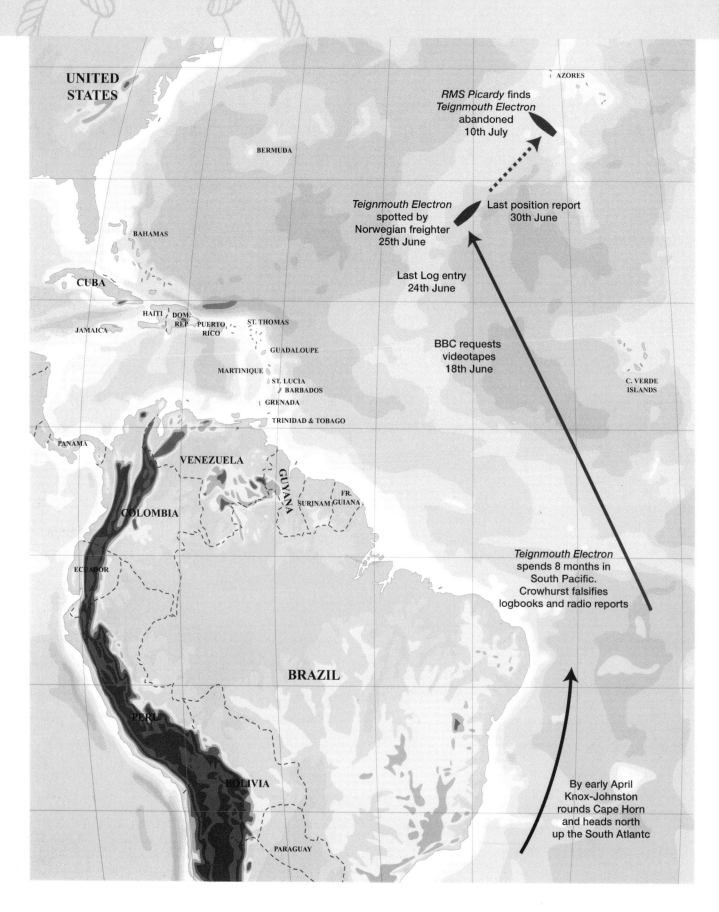

UNITED
STATES

AZORES

RMS Picardy finds
Teignmouth Electron
abandoned
10th July

BERMUDA

Teignmouth Electron
spotted by
Norwegian freighter
25th June

Last position report
30th June

BAHAMAS

Last Log entry
24th June

CUBA

HAITI
DOM.
REP
PUERTO
RICO
ST. THOMAS

JAMAICA

GUADALOUPE

BBC requests
videotapes
18th June

C. VERDE
ISLANDS

MARTINIQUE

ST. LUCIA
BARBADOS

GRENADA

TRINIDAD & TOBAGO

PANAMA

VENEZUELA

GUYANA
SURINAM
FR.
GUIANA

COLOMBIA

Teignmouth Electron
spends 8 months in
South Pacific.
Crowhurst falsifies
logbooks and radio reports

ECUADOR

BRAZIL

PERU

BOLIVIA

By early April
Knox-Johnston
rounds Cape Horn
and heads north
up the South Atlantc

PARAGUAY

Australia, Crowhurst seemed to be coming up fast behind the remaining yachtsmen, Bernard Moitessier and Nigel Tetley. During February Crowhurst reported making good progress, and by early March he was considered a possible winning contender, especially after Bernard Moitessier pulled out in mid-Pacific. Nobody expected Knox-Johnston's small yacht *Suhaili* to make it, so the press concentrated on the race between Crowhurst and Tetley. In fact, for a week or two everyone suspected the *Suhaili* had been lost rounding Cape Horn, but in early April Knox-Johnston was spotted by a tanker, heading up the South Atlantic toward Britain. He would be the first home, but as he took so long to complete the voyage, the prize for the fastest passage would go to either Tetley or Crowhurst. Radio messages from both Tetley and Crowhurst indicated they had successfully rounded Cape Horn, and were heading north behind Knox-Johnston. It seemed as if it really would be a race to the finish between the two men. Then, on May 21, Tetley's catamaran fell apart, forcing the yachtsman to abandon ship. Although he was rescued soon afterward, he was out of the race. All Crowhurst had to do now was to make it home and he would win the coveted prize.

On June 18, the BBC radioed him, asking for any videotape he'd taken during the voyage, to use in their celebratory broadcast. They suggested a pick-up by fast boat from the Azores. Crowhurst never replied. A week later on June 25, Crowhurst was sighted by a Norwegian freighter some 750 miles (1,200 km) south-west of the Azores. According to the crew he seemed in good health

Above: Donald Crowhurt (1932–69), in Teignmouth, preparing his boat for his round-the-world voyage.

and good spirits, waving at the crew of the passing ship. The following day his publicity agent called, telling him that upward of 100,000 people were expected to see him sail home into Teignmouth. Crowhurst responded cheerfully, then sent another position report on June 30. It was the last thing anyone heard from him. Ten days later, on July 10, 1969, the RMS *Picardy* sailing between Britain and the Caribbean came across the *Teignmouth Electron* creeping along under light sail. The captain of the *Picardy* hailed the yacht, but when there was no response he decided to lower a boat and investigate. The boarding party found the yacht deserted. Although there was no sign of Crowhurst, everything else seemed in good shape. There were dirty dishes in the galley, the parts of various radio receivers lay around on the table, and a stack of three logbooks sat on top of the chart table. The last logbook entry was for June 24, the day before Crowhurst was spotted by the Norwegian freighter. The last entry in the radio log was on June 29, the day before his last radio transmission. The yacht was winched aboard the *Picardy*, and her captain informed the British Navy and Lloyds of London about his discovery. He also requested a search to be made of the area, in case Crowhurst had fallen overboard but was still alive. Nothing was found. Meanwhile, Captain Box decided to read Crowhurst's logs and journals, to try to find out what had happened.

It was clear some tragedy had befallen the lone yachtsman, and the *Sunday Times* immediately launched an appeal fund for his family. Knox-Johnston generously donated his prize money of £5,000, and the *Sunday Times* matched the donation. The press speculated what had happened, and inevitably ran stories comparing the *Teignmouth Electron* to the *Mary Celeste*; they printed rumors that Crowhurst had reached South Africa, or the Cape Verde Islands, even Kent! Crowhurst's publicity agent, Rodney Hallworth, flew out to rendezvous with the *Picardy*, accompanied by the *Sunday Times* reporter Nicolas Tomalin, planning to recover the logbooks for a newspaper story. They were met by Captain Box who asked them to read the logs before deciding what they should do. As they read, the true story of Donald Crowhurst's amazing voyage was revealed.

He had kept two logbooks: one for the press and the other for himself. One described the progress he was supposed to have made in his circumnavigation; the other revealed that he had actually never left the Atlantic. Lagging behind the rest of the pack and in a boat whose seaworthiness he was beginning to doubt, Crowhurst decided to remain in the south-western Atlantic, far from any shipping lanes, where he planned to join on behind the others as they sailed home. That way he could save face, confound his critics, and return a hero. For nearly eight months he monitored the progress of the race by radio, sending in a series of positional reports which indicated he was still a contender; but he was suffering from the strain of being alone in a small yacht, with a very big secret on his conscience. His writings became progressively more garbled, so that by June when the race was supposedly reaching its climax, it seemed as if the solitary yachtsman had lost his sanity. Captain Box found some 25,000 words of closely-spaced, meaningless writing: a clear sign of someone under tremendous strain. By the time the Norwegian freighter sighted Crowhurst on June 25, he looked healthy enough from a distance, but he was a broken man. As the prospects of actually winning the race by default grew, his sense of guilt must have become overwhelming.

Many assumed that Donald Crowhurst was so consumed by his guilt that he stepped off his boat and offered himself up to the sea. Others are less convinced. If his intention was to commit suicide, why then did Crowhurst not leave a note to explain his actions, or even simply dispose of all the incriminating logbooks? His chronometer was missing, and it was presumed he held the instrument as he jumped overboard. This seems a strange act, even for a man who had lost his power of reason. He had also cut his hair before he disappeared, more the act of a man preparing himself to face the glare of publicity and inquiry than a man who planned to take his own life. His old yachting friends recalled how he was incredibly prone to falling overboard, or slipping between yacht and pier. It is therefore likely that the lone, mentally-shattered yachtsman simply fell overboard, probably knocking the chronometer overboard in the process. While the truth about Donald Crowhurst's final moments may never be known, the logbooks revealed the scale of his deception, and the agony he went through as the months passed. He was a brave, gifted man, and one who paid the ultimate price for his actions. Ironically after studying the evidence, men like Robin Knox-Johnston and Sir Francis Chichester praised Crowhurst's boat, and his maritime skills. If he had actually ran the race, he might not have come in first, but he would certainly have returned the hero he so desperately wished to be. As for the *Teignmouth Electron*, she was sold at auction and spent two decades as a fishing charter boat working out of Jamaica. She now lies abandoned in the Cayman Islands, her outriggers splintered by hurricanes and her paint peeling in the tropical sun.

Below: The remains of the *Teignmouth Electron* now lie on the shore of Cayman Brac in the Caribbean, a sad end to a once famous vessel.

ADRIFT IN THE PACIFIC:
THE *JOYITA* (1955)

The small motor vessel *Joyita* set sail from the South Sea island of Samoa on the morning of October 3, 1955. She was on a routine voyage to the Tokelau Islands, a trip that should have lasted two days at the most. She never arrived. A full-scale search was launched, but it appeared as if the boat had vanished without trace. Some 36 days later the boat was found drifting and abandoned off the Fiji archipelago, some hundreds of miles from her destination. There was no sign of the 25 people who sailed from Samoa on board her. Described as a modern-day *Mary Celeste*, the tale of the *Joyita* has defied all attempts to unravel the mystery. The deeper one looks into the case, the more perplexing the story becomes.

The *Joyita* began life as a private yacht, owned by the celebrated Hollywood director, and weekend sailor Roland West. In 1931 Roland left his wife for a pretty young actress, Thelma Todd (nicknamed "Hot Toddy" by the Hollywood press), and he made her the leading lady in his new gangster movie *The Corsair* (1931). Unfortunately both Miss Todd and *The Corsair* proved unpopular with the movie-going public, and West decided to retire from the business. To celebrate his new-found freedom he purchased a large motor yacht from the Wilmington Boat Works of Los Angeles, California, and named her *Joyita*, meaning "Little Jewel" in Spanish. She had been designed by the top pre-war West Coast boat designer Ted Geary. West fitted out the

> The *Joyita* began life as a private yacht, owned by the celebrated Hollywood director and weekend sailor Roland West. In 1931 Roland left his wife for a pretty young actress, Thelma Todd, and he made her the leading lady in his new gangster movie *The Corsair* (1931).

75-foot (23-m), 70-ton boat as the perfect pleasure boat, with a luscious interior, a well-appointed galley, and even large chairs in her stern for deep-sea fishing. Over the next few years Roland West and Thelma Todd spent a lot of time on the boat, fishing off Catalina Island, and throwing lavish parties on board. The story ended in tragedy in 1935, when Thelma Todd was found dead in her car, after being beaten unconscious, then asphyxiated by carbon dioxide. Roland West was the prime suspect, although his involvement in the murder was never proven. He sold the boat and skipped town, the transaction being so sudden that West still hadn't cleared out all of Miss Todd's effects from the *Joyita*'s stateroom. The new owner was Californian businessman

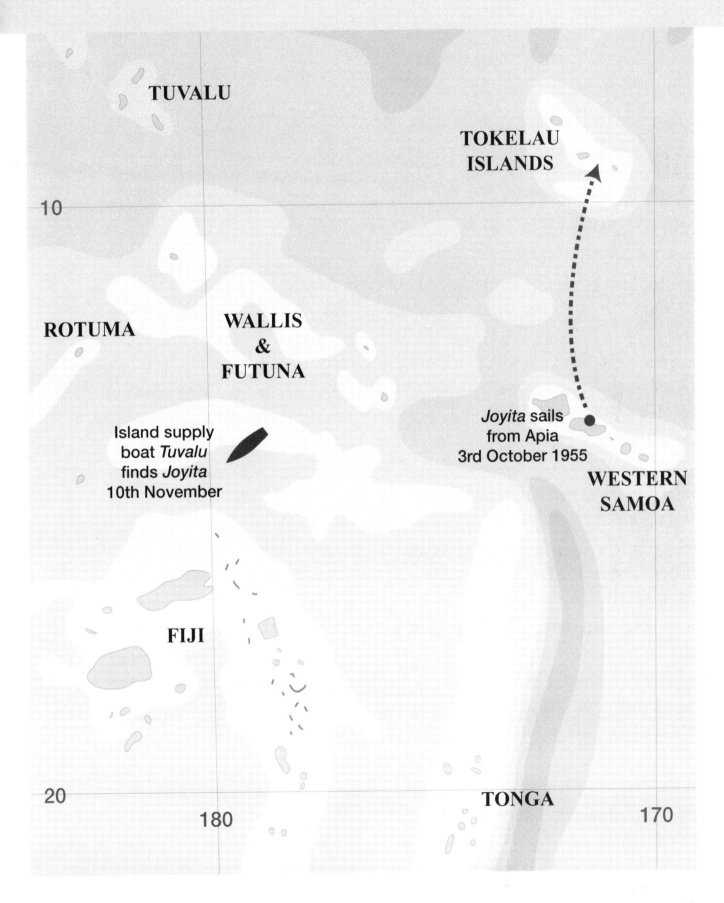

TUVALU

TOKELAU
ISLANDS

10

ROTUMA

WALLIS
&
FUTUNA

Joyita sails
from Apia
3rd October 1955

Island supply
boat *Tuvalu*
finds *Joyita*
10th November

WESTERN
SAMOA

FIJI

20

TONGA

180

170

Miller needed something to happen fast, as he was reduced to doing odd jobs on the island in return for money to eat. He was also too proud to confess to Dr. Luomala that he was in such dire straits. However, Pearless finally won through, and the *Joyita* was chartered to make the trip.

Milton E. Bacon, who was reputedly no sailor, but liked spending time on board her as a form of escape from work. Like many large motor yachts, after the Japanese attack on Pearl Harbor the *Joyita* was requisitioned by the US Navy, and she was converted into a lightly-armed patrol boat. The *Joyita* suffered the indignity of becoming a SP (Section Patrol Craft), one of hundreds of un-named boats pressed into service to close harbor boom nets, or transfer stores. In 1943 she ran aground off Pearl Harbor, causing some damage, but otherwise she had an uneventful war. In 1946 the Marine Commission sold her to a company who turned her into a fishing boat. The Louis Brothers of Honolulu gutted her, converting her hold to a fish storage freezer. At the same time the inside of her hull was lined with five inches of cork, which served both as insulation for the freezers, and made the boat virtually unsinkable. Her

engines were replaced with reliable modern diesels, and fishing winches were installed on her decks, where the deep-sea fishing chairs had once stood. They used her as a deep-sea fishing boat, working out of both Hawaii and Samoa, and by the early 1950s the once elegant pleasure boat had become the roughest of work boats. In 1953 they sold the *Joyita* to Dr. Katharine Luomala, an anthropology lecturer at the University of Hawaii, who chartered her to former British naval officer Thomas "Dusty" Miller. Rumor had it that Miller was Luomala's partner, although apparently he still had an estranged wife back in Britain. Dusty Miller was a colorful character; hard-drinking ashore, but the perfect boat captain when he was afloat. While he had a reputation as something of a rogue, he was also respected as a good seaman. After three less than successful fishing trips he headed south toward Samoa. He arrived in Apia on Western Samoa in July 1954 with the *Joyita*'s freezers full of rotting fish: the cooling system had failed while he was at sea. Miller was out of money, so following Dr. Luomala's advice he tried to sell the boat to the Fijian government. The offer was declined, leaving Miller struggling to pay his harbor dues. Then his luck seemed to change. In late March he met Roger Pearless, a 29-year-old District Officer from New Zealand, who was looking for ways of establishing a reliable link between Western Samoa and his outpost in the Tokelau Islands, some 270 miles (432 km) to the north. The two men discussed chartering the *Joyita* for an annual run between the two island groups, and on March 25, Peerless chartered the boat for a dummy-run, a month-long fishing trip off the Tokelau group. Miller and Pearless became friends during the expedition, and on their return to port Pearless took the annual charter proposal to his superiors. The Tokelau Islands wanted to export copra, the coconut meat used to make oil, in exchange for foodstuffs and medical supplies. Therefore Pearless approached E.A. Coxon & Co., a local copra company to fund the charter. Miller needed something to happen fast, as he was reduced to doing odd jobs on the island in return for money to eat. He was also too proud to confess to Dr. Luomala that he was in such dire straits. However, Pearless finally won through, and

the *Joyita* was chartered to make the trip. The only stipulation the copra people had was that the *Joyita* should be able to carry two passengers as well as supplies and copra. A delighted Captain Miller was only too happy to agree. With the promise of money, he set about hiring a crew. Local Gilbert Island seamen Tekoka and Tanini had sailed with him before as mate and engineer respectively, while Miller also hired the American seaman Chuck Simpson, or "Captain Jah" as bosun, and together these men managed to find another dozen Samoans to serve as deckhands. Although the *Joyita* was uninsured and her engines were in need of an

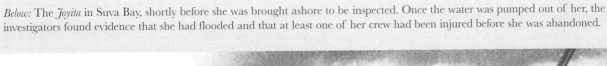

Below: The *Joyita* in Suva Bay, shortly before she was brought ashore to be inspected. Once the water was pumped out of her, the investigators found evidence that she had flooded and that at least one of her crew had been injured before she was abandoned.

> Miller simply took as much as his boat could carry. He did the same trick with food supplies, filling two of his freezers and taking on board 2,500 gallons of fresh water. Whatever happened, the *Joyita* was well-stocked for the voyage.

overhaul, Miller had managed to scrape together enough crew to fulfil his charter obligations. Probably the fact that the *Joyita* was virtually unsinkable might have helped sway any doubters on the island. "Captain Jah" was a particularly lucky find, as officially the *Joyita* was an American-registered vessel, and therefore she needed to have an American officer on board. While Miller was no stickler for marine regulations, he probably wanted to give the appearance of compliance. Miller was also able to arrange for the supply of fuel on credit, a full load of some 2,640 gallons of diesel, which was enough to make the return trip five times over. Much was later made of this, but more than likely when faced with the opportunity of obtaining fuel on credit, Miller simply took as much as his boat could carry. He did the same trick with food supplies, filling two of his freezers, and taking on board 2,500 gallons of fresh

water. Whatever happened, the *Joyita* was well-stocked for the voyage.

In late September the passengers and cargo began to arrive on the dock in Apia. Pearlson loaded the cases of food and medical supplies. The two copra company passengers then arrived, Messrs. Wallwork and Williams, both of whom were entered into the books as "supercargos," as Miller had no official license to carry passengers. Williams took a small case on board with him, containing just under £1,000 in Samoan currency to pay for the copra. As part of his middle-man deal between the islanders and the copra traders, Pearson also brought his own people, Irish-born Dr. Andy Parsons from the local Samoan hospital, and Mr. Hodgkinson, his pharmacist. Finally seven Tokelau Islanders joined the boat, four men, one woman, and two children. All of them had been waiting for months for a ride home.

Finally everything was ready. Almost an hour before noon on Sunday October 2, the *Joyita* slipped from the dock, and headed out of the harbor. Suddenly there was a thump, a cloud of smoke, and the engines stopped, leaving the boat drifting toward the reefs which lined the harbor entrance. Miller managed to throw down an anchor, and disaster was averted. This mechanical failure was hardly an auspicious start to the voyage, and the passengers were off-loaded while Miller and Tanini struggled to repair the damaged port engine clutch. The following night the passengers re-embarked, to discover that the repair had been makeshift; the clutch was partially disengaged, but at least the repair

Above: Captain Douglas of the MV *Tuvalu* towed the *Joyita* into the harbor of Suva in the Fiji Islands where the authorities could conduct a thorough investigation into her disappearance and abandonment.

allowed them to continue with the voyage. Miller was also keen to get underway, before anyone questioned the reliability of his boat to undertake the charter, or he became embroiled in any questions about marine regulations with the port authorities. This time the *Joyita* slipped out of port all but unobserved, leaving at 5 am on October 3. The whole incident had probably unsettled both the passengers and crew alike, and they all must have been wondering what would happen if the *Joyita* should break down somewhere in mid-ocean. The last anyone on Samoa saw of her was as she disappeared over the horizon to the north, lit by the dawning sun. Captain Miller, his passengers and his crew were never seen again.

If the *Joyita* had steamed at a steady 10–12 knots, she would have arrived during the early hours of Tuesday morning. However, as dawn broke on October 4, there was no sign of her. Nobody was unduly concerned, but by that evening the islanders had begun to worry. By Wednesday evening it was clear that something had gone wrong, and the authorities on Samoa were notified. On the morning of Thursday October 6, a Royal New Zealand Air Force Sunderland flying boat left its base at Fiji, then flew to Apia before searching the route between Samoa and the Tokelaus. Despite good visibility and surface search-radar, there was no sign of the missing boat. A small storm was passing through the area, and the *Joyita* would have

Left: The *Joyita* as she was discovered by the crew of the *Tuvalu* on November 10, 1955. The temporary awning rigged over her damaged wheelhouse can be clearly seen. Only her lining of cork kept the vessel afloat long enough for her to be discovered.

encountered rough seas during her voyage, the prelude to worse weather to come. The storm blew itself out over the next few days, but the choppy seas still made a visual search difficult, as it was hard to spot a small boat on a stormy ocean. For the next five days after the initial search more planes joined the sweep, covering an area of almost 100,000 square miles (259,000 sq km) of ocean. The search area extended out on both sides of the *Joyita*'s intended course, but the air crews concentrated their attentions to the west, which was the likely direction the vessel would have drifted if her engines had failed. Passing shipping and aircraft were radioed to keep a lookout for the *Joyita*, and all emergency radio channels were monitored. No message came, and nobody spotted any boat or wreckage. It seemed as if the *Joyita* had simply vanished without trace. On October 12, the search was called off, and the boat was officially listed as missing.

Then, just before 7 am on November 10 Captain Douglas of the island supply boat *Tuvalu* radioed a morse code message to the authorities at Suva on the Fiji Islands. He reported: "The *Joyita* found waterlogged in position 14°42' S, 179°45' E (by dead reckoning). Boat sent across but nobody found on board but possibility in flooded compartments. Port side superstructure including funnel blown or washed away. Canvas awning rigged apparently subsequent to accident. No log book or message found." Although the boat had been found, the mystery deepened.

That was when the rumors started. The press fell upon the story, and even before the *Joyita* was towed into

Despite good visibility and surface search radar, there was no sign of the missing boat. A small storm was passing through the area, and the *Joyita* would have encountered rough seas during her voyage, the prelude to worse weather to come.

Suva, headlines had appeared, describing her as the new *Mary Celeste*. She had been drifting about 160 miles (256 km) north of Fiji, and some 650 miles (1,040 km) south-west of her original destination. When Captain Douglas found the *Joyita*, she was riding very low in the water and listing heavily to port, with her port side deck awash. Her bows were pointing west, and although her hull was undamaged, her superstructure had been battered, the flying bridge caved in and her deck fittings buckled and smashed. Mysteriously, a canvas awning had been rigged over her deckhouse. Barnacles and marine growth on her hull suggested she had been listing for weeks, and Douglas felt the hull damage was consistent with a boat which had been abandoned and left to drift in the pounding swell for that long.

New Zealand airman Gerry Ayre was one of the first men to clamber aboard her when she reached

The radio was set to the local distress frequency, but a break was discovered in the aerial, which had been covered over with paint. This meant that the range of the transmitter was limited to just a few miles.

Suva: "Sgt. Frankie Doyle, Flt. Lt. Armfelt and myself were the first to board this vessel when she was towed into Fiji. It was scary opening hatches etc, looking for some sign of the missing 12 people or so who should have been on board her. We found nothing, not even a scrap of paper or a pencil. She was clean, no rags, no nothing." The authorities then examined her more thoroughly. This inspection raised far more questions than it answered. Whatever disaster had befallen the vessel, it happened at night. The clock on board was stopped at 10:25 pm, and the navigation lights were switched on. There were clear signs of serious engine failure; one engine showing signs of emergency repairs, while the other was smothered with four mattresses. Almost all useful objects which could be removed were missing from the ship, while there was no sign of the *Joyita's* three life rafts; a 16-man one, two ten-man floats, and a dingy fitted with an outboard engine. The air

search was resumed, but no sign of the missing rafts were found. It was then discovered that the dinghy had been left behind in Apia when the vessel sailed. Captain Miller knew that the cork fitted around the inside of the *Joyita's* hull meant that his vessel was virtually unsinkable. Although her hull was mysteriously filled with water, the vessel's passengers and crew would have been relatively safe on her upper decks thanks to the cork. Her freezers were filled with provisions, so if the engines did break down, then why was she abandoned? Why was no note left in case the abandoned vessel was discovered. Who had rigged the awning, and why?

When the water was pumped out the investigators found that an auxiliary pump had been rigged in the engine room, lashed to a balk of timber lying athwart the two engines. While it was clearly designed to operate a pump, there was no sign that it had ever been operated. The port engine clutch was found to be disconnected, most probably the result of the makeshift repairs made to the engine before the *Joyita* sailed from Apia. That evening the assistant harbormaster at Suva heard water trickling into the hull, and he searched for the source. He discovered that water was pouring into the bilges through a one-inch (2.54 cm) diameter pipe, located well below the waterline, and under the deckboards. It was part of the ship's cooling system, and the brass head on the pipe had corroded and broken off. This meant that water had only one place to go, which was into the ship. When the ship was underway, the noise of the engines would have drowned out the sound of the gushing water, and the first Miller and his crew would know of the flood was when water began to cover the deckboards in the engine room.

The next day the investigation continued. The radio was set to the local distress frequency, but a break was discovered in the aerial, which had been covered over with paint. This meant that the range of the transmitter was limited to just a few miles. The mystery of why there was no distress signal was answered, as too was the *Joyita* had not been located by airborne radar. As the boat was of all-wood construction, she was difficult to spot on radar. The search aircraft had probably flown close overhead, but failed to spot her on their radar screens.

The next discovery was even more mysterious. A doctor's bag was found, complete with a scalpel, needles, and gut for sutures, and a length of bloodstained bandage. Clearly this was Doctor Parson's bag, but who had he treated for an injury, and whose blood was on the bandage? The prime candidate was Captain Miller. If he had been knocked unconscious, the passengers

Below: When the sailors from the MV *Tuvalu* found the *Joyita* abandoned and drifting north of the Fiji Islands, the vessel's master Captain Douglas radioed the news to the local authorities, ending one mystery and beginning another.

and crew might have not known about the "unsinkable" nature of the boat, and might have taken to the life rafts in an emergency. However, this was just speculation, one of the many assumptions and theories which were being made by locals and newsmen alike. What was just as perplexing was not what was found on board, but what was no longer there. For some reason the cargo was missing; seven cases of aluminium strips (used by the Tokelau islanders to keep rodents off their coconut trees), 15 sacks of sugar, 11 sacks of rice, and 460 empty sacks belonging to the copra company. In addition Mr. Williams' money was missing; the money he planned to buy the islander's copra with. If the passengers and crew had taken to the boats in an emergency, then what happened to the cargo? The life rafts were barely large enough to hold the survivors, leaving no room for the cargo.

By this time the newspapers were seizing on every new scrap of information, and readers were willing to believe even the most outlandish hypotheses. One theory was that the *Joyita* had fallen foul of an underwater quake, a geological event which was uncommon but not unknown in the area. However, this failed to explain why there were no survivors. Another theory centered around the discovery of a charred door to a cabin on board, and foul play was suspected, until someone remembered that this damage to the *Joyita* pre-dated the boat's last voyage, the result of a fire on board earlier in the year. Others thought she had been hit by a larger waterspout, or a tidal wave, or even a freak squall. None of these phenomena explained away the other

questions, like the disappearance of the cargo, or the fact that someone had remained on board the disabled boat long enough to rig an awning. Whatever happened, the crew had some warning, and had time to transfer supplies or people into the life rafts. This left the possibility of foul play. Smugglers, drug-runners, modern-day pirates or even a rogue Japanese submarine were all considered, but it was not until just before Christmas when the *Fiji Times and Herald* ran the headline "All aboard *Joyita* murdered" that this option was even considered a real possibility. The story claimed that the boat had probably run into a Japanese fishing fleet which had been spotted in the area around the time the *Joyita* disappeared. It blamed the fishermen, suggesting that they had attacked the *Joyita*, killed the passengers and crew, then looted the cargo. It claimed that the Japanese fleet's mother ship, the *Koyo Maru* was equipped with the latest radar, and could easily have tracked down and overpowered the American-registered boat. Worse, the paper even hinted that this was the official line being pursued by the New Zealand authorities charged with investigating the mystery. The authorities were quick to deny the story, and the Colonial Secretary of Fiji even made a radio announcement denying there was any official line, let alone one which blamed the Japanese.

The *Joyita* mystery also attracted its share of cranks. An Australian lay cleric contacted the Fijian government, claiming that everyone from the *Joyita* was still alive, and had been miraculously transported to the Solomon Islands. Meanwhile an Australian clairvoyant

The *Joyita* mystery also attracted its share of cranks. An Australian lay cleric contacted the Fijian government, claiming that everyone from the *Joyita* was still alive, and had been miraculously transported to the Solomon Islands.

claimed that she had been in contact with the dead crew, who had revealed that a drum of gunpowder had exploded, setting off a glycerine container which blew a hole in the side of the ship. Unfortunately her theory failed to explain how the hull had miraculously patched itself up, as only the superstructure of the boat was actually damaged, and that was caused by wave rather than explosive power!

It was hoped that the Board of Inquiry into the disaster would help to end the rumors, but instead the hearing turned into a courtroom drama, with the press eagerly awaiting any new piece of evidence which could add a new twist to the tale. The Board of Inquiry was convened in Apia on Western Samoa on February 3, 1956, and the hearing was presided over by Judge Carsack, of the New Zealand judiciary, a man appointed by the New Zealand High Commission in

Samoa. The first batch of witnesses included the harbormaster Commander Plowman and Kurt von Reiche, manager of the copra company. Both testified that the departure of the *Joyita* was delayed due to engine problems, and that Miller had probably sailed with one engine disconnected. Plowman also revealed that the vessel wasn't licensed to carry passengers, and that he had doubts about her radio. Miller managed to convince him that both problems would be taken care of, then sailed before Plowman could inspect the boat more thoroughly. Miller needed the money the charter would bring, and couldn't afford to risk losing the contract through faulty equipment or paperwork. Miller was also found responsible for not sailing with a working radio, proper lifesaving equipment, or with engines that could be relied upon.

A string of witnesses then described the technical problems with the *Joyita*, the reason she had become flooded, and suggested a sequence of events which explained her mechanical and electrical breakdowns. As the water flooded into the boat through the faulty pipe, the engines had stopped working, and the mattresses had probably been used as a way of prolonging their life, keeping the rising water at bay in the hope that the electric pumps could turn the tide. Once the engines failed, the boat would have turned broadside onto the waves and rolled alarmingly. Only the buoyancy provided by her cork lining would have kept her afloat, although she would have been riding extremely low in the water. It seemed Miller's belief in the unsinkable nature of his boat made him consider the risks he faced

> The inquiry concerned itself with the technical aspects of this disaster, not the human ones. It was unable to explain what had happened to everyone on board the *Joyita*, or explain the blood-soaked bandages.

to be acceptable. The final ruling was that he had put to sea in an unsafe vessel, and that when the *Joyita* broke down her power had gone, and she was left drifting. The damage to the superstructure was consistent with a vessel which had been battered by the waves for weeks on end after she had been abandoned. As for the lack of any human life, this was explained by the passengers and crew deciding to abandon ship, although the subsequent fate of these survivors remained a mystery.

The inquiry concerned itself with the technical aspects of this disaster, not the human ones. It was unable to explain what had happened to everyone on board the *Joyita*, or explain away the blood-soaked bandages. As the report put it, they regarded "the fate of the passengers and crew as inexplicable on the evidence submitted at the inquiry." The press were more than happy to fill in the gaps. They hinted that the harbormaster thought the inquiry was a sham, designed to cover up something the authorities were hiding. After all, the *Joyita* was hired by a government official, and the

New Zealand government might have been held responsible for the lives which were presumably lost. Another theory the papers developed was that Miller had hijacked his own boat, and had set course for Honolulu against the wishes of his fellow travelers. This was extremely unlikely, as circumstantial evidence suggested Miller had expected to be back in Apia within a few days. It would also have been near impossible for one man to force 24 other people to sail somewhere against their will. Other sailors in Apia vouched for Miller, claiming that he would never have abandoned his vessel voluntarily. This tended to suggest the blood on the bandages belonged to the captain.

Had Miller been in a fight, and knocked unconscious before being taken on board the rafts? Had he been injured trying to save his ship? Was the ship attacked by another vessel, and the bodies simply fed to the sharks? There were simply more theories than there were newpapers to print them. After the inquiry the speculation subsided, but never completely went away. Every few years a fresh rumor would circulate, and the press would pick up the story again. In July 1956 Dr. Luomala sold the boat to a Fijian planter, who later claimed the *Joyita* was haunted. Claiming she was unlucky, he had her beached, and abandoned her.

In 1960 the hulk was bought by the British novelist Lord Robert Maugham, the nephew of Somerset Maugham. The young aristocrat became fascinated by the story, and even wrote a book about her, where he suggested that the *Joyita* had broken down, then Miller was knocked unconscious when the boat rolled in heavy seas. The passengers and crew abandoned her, leaving the engineer Tanini to tend to his captain and to try to pump out the water and fix the engines. Maugham then surmised that Miller had died before Tanini, and the Japanese fishermen had found the drifting boat, then looted it. As dead men tell no tales, Tanini was killed and thrown overboard, along with Miller.

This dramatic version of events was of course pure conjecture. Who knows what happened on board the boat. Why would Miller have been left behind? Why was there no trace of the life rafts? Why did none of the Japanese fishermen ever come clean and tell their side of the story? Another version of the tale developed in 1958, after six skeletons were found in a cave on Henderson Island, some 2,000 miles (3,200 km) away. It was suggested these bodies were the last of the *Joyita's* survivors. Unfortunately no further evidence was found to back up the notion, and the bodies remain unidentified. More likely the remains were those of Polynesian islanders, who traditionally buried their dead in remote caves. The Henderson Island skeletons have remained something of a mystery ever since.

Another simpler explanation was also bandied about. If Miller was badly injured when the wave smashed in the boat's superstructure, the remaining passengers and crew would have been unaware that the boat was virtually unsinkable. If everyone including Miller took to the life rafts, the *Joyita* would have been left to drift. If then the Japanese had come across the abandoned boat, they would have treated her as legitimate salvage, and taken what they could of her cargo. However, this fails to explain why no fisherman ever mentioned encountering the *Joyita*, especially during the media frenzy erupted when the boat was discovered.

While the intervening decades have served to dampen interest in the *Joyita* mystery, they have also failed to bring any answers to the puzzle. A new book published in 2002 by New Zealand lecturer David Wright, a relative of Roger Pearless, the Tokelau District Officer, came up with a new solution to the mystery. Wright blamed Miller for the disaster, and offered his own version of events. However, like all previous attempts at solving the mystery, his version is at best just educated speculation. Probably nobody will ever know what happened after the *Joyita* set sail that morning almost half a century ago, and like so many other nautical mysteries, the sea will keep her secrets.

THE ABIDING ATTRACTION
OF SEA MYSTERIES

In the early 21st century we have access to technology which a mariner a century ago could never have imagined. To the sailors who fought at the Battle of Trafalgar in 1805, the steamships used by the sailors of the Edwardian Age would have seemed like something from another world. Maritime technology has moved quickly in the past two centuries, and even more so in the past two decades. Today even the smallest yacht is capable of carrying a compact GPS system which uses satellite tracking, and which can fix its position anywhere on the planet to within an inch. While even 20 years ago many ships had to rely on Decca systems and navigational radar to fix their position, now anyone can do it at the press of a button. Today most merchant ships have auto-navigation aids, electronically-monitored mechanisms, and computer-assisted engine-control systems. Maritime travel is therefore far safer now than it ever was.

However, ships still run aground, or sink in mid-ocean, and even disappear without a trace. Being a sailor is still one of the most dangerous jobs around. In its 1999 report the International Labour Organisation reported that an average of 24,000 fisherman die every year around the world. Many of these deaths represent careless accidents, while others reflect the risks taken by Third World fishermen sailing in primitive craft in areas without efficient rescue services, or who encounter the worst nature has to offer: tsunamis, tropical storms, cyclones, typhoons, and hurricanes. It also includes a number of cases where larger fishing boats are lost at sea. Undoubtedly, many of these losses are caused by human error, lack of knowledge, or the result of economic pressure on fishermen to cut corners, but some remain more of a mystery.

An example of this is provided by the British trawler *Gaul*, a Hull-based vessel which was lost off Norway's North Cape on February 7, 1974. The area was being swept by a bad winter gale, and waves of up to 50 feet (15 m) were reported. Still, the *Gaul* was a well-built ship, and she was designed to operate in just these conditions. Still she foundered. In the months which followed there was intense speculation whether the ship was a victim of the storm, or had been accidentally or even deliberately rammed and sunk by a warship or submarine. During the Cold War these hostile waters were the maritime front line between East and West, and the *Gaul* was operating in waters patrolled by the well-armed fleets of both sides. Another rumor suggested that the *Gaul* was deliberately sunk by the Russians as she was secretly operating as a spy ship, a claim rigorously denied by all other parties. Such is the nature of unexplained ship losses that almost every conceivable theory will emerge to explain what happened, and many unconceivable ones as well. As the

Above: The oil tanker SS *Watertown* was at sea in December 1924, sailing from the Pacific coast of America to the Panama Canal, when two men died in an accident and were buried at sea. The next day and for many days following, two phantom faces were reportedly seen to be following the ship. Was there a logical explanation, or was some supernatural force at work?

sea usually swallows up the evidence, theorists are free to speculate as much as they like.

That is the abiding fascination with mysteries of the sea, with phantom ships and abandoned vessels, with monsters of the deep, and ships supposedly bearing a curse. As the sea remains a hostile, largely misunderstood environment, it also takes on a sinister quality. This means that we are more likely to consider a wider range of theories to help explain these unexplained events than we would if a similar mystery had taken place on land. The ocean remains a place of latent power, and of brooding sinister potential. Milton described the seas which surround us in his epic poem "Paradise Lost:" "A dark illimitable ocean without bound, without dimension, where length, breadth and height, where time and place are lost." The oceans will always be mysterious, regardless of how powerful we feel behind the shield of modern technology. For that reason we will always be fascinated by the secrets it still withholds from us.

EXPLORING THE MYSTERY

Clearly it isn't always possible to jump in a submersible and search the oceans for ships like the *Waratah*, the *Cyclops* or the *Københaven*, although some people are doing exactly that: devoting their time and resources to tracking down these ships and solving the mysteries. If this seems a little excessive, then there are plenty of other ways to achieve similar ends without the expense and danger. For example, many of the maritime mysteries, ghost stories, nautical disasters, and tales of phantom ships are all works in progress. What you've read represents the state of knowledge as we know it. Things could change dramatically as a new piece of evidence is brought to light, a persistent rumor is irrevocably debunked or a new lead is unearthed. For example, in the account of the haunting of HMS *Asp*, nobody has been able to identify the mysterious woman

whose ghost reputedly haunted the ship from 1850 until 1857. Through some diligent detective work in museums, archives, and church records, the information may one day come to light, and another piece of the puzzle will be found. It might explain how she was killed (if she was at all), why her ghost reportedly threw furniture around, and kept pointing towards the sky. There must be clues out there, just waiting to be found.

For those without the spare time or the inclination to become ghost hunters, you can find out even more about the subject by visiting the places listed opposite, or simply just browsing some of the diverse websites. Failing that, there's an extensive list of relevant books covering all aspects of nautical mysteries, ghost ships, and even sea monsters in the bibliography, most of which are available in any good library.

Right: The wreck of the USS *Maine* in Havana Harbor.

SHIPS AND PLACES TO VISIT

While most of the ships mentioned in the book are no longer with us, a surprising handful still exist, or traces of them can still be found. For example, the bell from HMS *Eurydice* is still hanging in the church in Shanklin, while the hurricane-battered hull of the *Teignmouth Electron* is still lying on the beach in Cayman Brac. You can still walk down the passageways of the RMS *Queen Mary* in Long Beach, and you can even see the relics left by the Franklin expedition in the National Maritime Museum in Greenwich, London. There is a permanent *Titanic* exhibition at the Maritime Museum of the Atlantic in Halifax, Nova Scotia, Canada, featuring relics from the ship. Three of the town's cemeteries feature the black granite headstones of 150 of the ship's victims. After its salvage from Havana harbor in 1911, relics of the USS *Maine* were distributed throughout the USA. One of the bow anchors was presented to the City of Reading, Pennsylvania and it can be found on display in the main city park on 6th Street. The mainmast is held by Arlington National Cemetery in Arlington, Virginia, while the foremast resides at the Naval Academy at Annapolis, Maryland. The stern scrollwork nameplate can be found in the Smithsonian Institute, Museum of American History in Washington D.C., the Conning Tower Base in Canton, Ohio. There is a Capstan at the Silver Bow County Courthouse, Butte, Montana and also one in Battery Park, Charleston, South Carolina. There is a six-pound gun in Munjoy Hill, Portland, Maine and a one-pound gun in Milford Park, Milford, Maine. There are also many other USS *Maine* relics around the country, including a turret sighting hood located in Mallory Square, Key West, Florida.

A selection of superb museums with relevant collections or displays are listed below.

National Maritime Museum, Greenwich, London
www.nmm.ac.uk

Royal Naval Museum, Portsmouth, Hampshire
www.royalnavalmuseum.org

Peabody-Essex Museum, Salem, Massachusetts
www.pem.org

Deutsches Schiffahrtsmuseum, Bremerhaven
(German Maritime Museum)
www.dsm.de

North Carolina Maritime Museum, Beaufort, North Carolina
www.ah.dcr.state.nc.us/sections/maritime/default.htm

Mel Fisher Maritime Museum, Key West, Florida
www.melfisher.org

RMS Queen Mary, Long Beach, California
www.queenmary.com

SOME USEFUL WEB SITES

Shipwrecks of the Steam Era
**www.rmstitanichistory.com/shipwrecks/
shipwrecks.html**

Mary Celeste: Fact, not Fiction
www.maryceleste.net

Joshua Slocum
www.joshuaslocumsocietyintl.org

Investigator Magazine
www.adam.com.au/bstett

Immigrant Ships
www.theshipslist.com

Occultopedia: An Encyclopaedia of the Occult
www.occultopedia.com

The SS *Waratah*
www.numa.co.za/sswaratah.htm

The Franklin Expedition
**www.canadiangeographic.ca/specialfeatures/
franklinexpedition**

The *Teignmouth Electron*
www.teignmouthelectron.org

The Bermuda Triangle
www.bermuda-triangle.org

The Blue Water Navy (US Navy Site)
www.navalships.org

Ghost Ships
www.gettysburgghosts.net/ghostships.htm

Ghost Ships of the Great Lakes
www.prairieghosts.com/glgship.html

"Crystal Links" Metaphysics and Science Site
www.crystalinks.com

Mary Celeste: The Seaquake Theory
www.deafwhale.com/maryceleste

THE PHANTOM SHIP
-Henry Wadsworth Longfellow-

In Mather's Magnalia Christi,
Of the old colonial time,
May be found in prose the legend
That is here set down in rhyme.

A ship sailed from New Haven,
And the keen and frosty airs,
That filled her sails in parting
Were heavy with good men's prayers.

"O Lord! If it be thy pleasure"-
Thus prayed the old divine-
"To bury our friends in the ocean,
Take them, for they are thine!"

But Master Lamberton muttered,
And under his breath said he,
"This ship is so crank and walty
I fear our grave she will be!"

And the ships that came from England
When the winter months were gone,
Brought no tidings of this vessel!
Nor of Master Lamberton.

This put the people to praying
That the Lord would let them hear
What in his greater wisdom
He had done to friends so dear.

And at last our prayers were answered:
It was in the month of June
An hour before sunset
Of a windy afternoon.

When, steadily steering landward,
A ship was seen below,
And they knew it was Lamberton, Master,
Who sailed so long ago.

On she came with a cloud of canvas,
Right against the wind that blew,
Until the eye could distinguish
The faces of the crew.

Then fell her straining top mast,
Hanging tangled in the shrouds,
And her sails were loosened and lifted,
And blown away like clouds.

And the masts, with all their rigging,
Fell slowly, one by one,
And the hulk dilated and vanished,
As a sea-mist in the sun!

And the people who saw thus marvel
Each said unto his friend,
That this was the mould of their vessel,
And thus her tragic end.

And the pastor of the village
Gave thanks to God in Prayer,
That, to quiet their troubled spirits,
He had sent this Ship of Air.

INDEX

BIBLIOGRAPHY

Armstrong, Warren; *Last Voyage* (London, 1958)

Armstrong, Warren; *Sea Phantoms* (London, 1964)

Barnaby, K.; *Some ship disasters and their causes* (London, 1968)

Beke, G.; *Titanic: Psychic forewarnings of a tragedy* (New York, 1986)

Berlitz, Charles; *The Bermuda Triangle Mystery* (New York, 1974)

Breed, Bryan; *Famous Mysteries of the Sea* (London, 1965)

Emmerson, G.S.; *SS Great Eastern* (Newton Abbot, 1980)

Fay, Charles E.; *Mary Celeste: The Odyssey of an abandoned ship* (Salem, 1942)

Garnett, Richard; *Voyage into Mystery* (London, 1987)

Harris, John; *Without Trace* (London, 1981)

Hastings, Macdonald; *Mary Celeste: A Centenary Record* (London, 1972)

Heuvelmans, B.; *In the wake of the Sea Serpents* (London, 1968)

Hicks, Brian; *Ghost Ship: The mysterious true story of the Mary Celeste* (London, 2004)

Hoehling, A.; *They sailed into oblivion* (London, 1959)

Keating, Lawrence J.; *The Great Mary Celeste Hoax* (London, 1921)

Kemp, Peter (ed.); *The Oxford Companion to Ships and the Sea* (Oxford, 1976)

Konstam, Angus; *The History of Shipwrecks* (New York, 1999)

Kusche, Lawrence D.; *The Bermuda Triangle Mystery – Solved* (New York, 1975)

Lamont-Brown, Raymond; *Phantoms, Legends and Customs of the Sea* (London, 1972)

Landström, Björn; *The Ship: An Illustrated History* (New York, 1961)

Larn, Richard; *Shipwrecks of Great Britain and Ireland* (London, 1981)

Lockhart, J.G.; *Mysteries of the Sea* (London, 1924)

Lockhart, J.G.; *Strange Adventures of the Sea* (London, 1929)

Lockhart, J.G.; *The Mary Celeste and other strange tales of the sea* (St. Albans, 1952)

McEwan G.J.; *Sea Serpents, Sailors & Sceptics* (London, 1978)

MacDougall, Philip; *Mysteries on the High Seas* (London, 1984)

MacDougall, Philip; *Phantoms on the High Seas* (London, 1988)

Markham, Captain A.H.; *Life of Sir John Franklin* (London, 1889)

Masters, David; *When ships go down* (London, 1936)

Maugham, Robert; *The Joyita Mystery* (London, 1962)

Mielke, Otto; *Disaster at Sea* (New York, 1958)

O'Donnell, Elliott; *Strange Sea Mysteries* (London, 1956)

O'Donnell, Elliot; *Haunted Waters* (London, 1957)

Ortzen, Len; *Strange Mysteries of the Sea* (London, 1976)

Paine, Lincoln; *Ships of the World: An Historical Encyclopaedia* (1997)

Slocum, Joshua; *Sailing alone around the world* (New York, 1900)

Snow, E.R.; *Unsolved Mysteries of the Sea* (London, 1964)

Spicer, Stanley T.; *The Saga of the Mary Celeste* (New York, 2002)

Tomalin, Nicolas & Hall, Ron; *The strange case of Donald Crowhurst* (New York, 1970)

Winer, Richard; *The Devil's Triangle* (New York, 1974)

Winer, Richard; *From the Devil's Triangle to the Devil's Jaw* (New York, 1974)

Woodman, Richard; *The History of the Ship* (London, 1997)

Wright, David G.; *Joyita: Solving the Mystery* (Auckland, 2002)